# Essays by Divers Hands

VOLUME XXXV

# Essays by Divers Hands

BEING THE TRANSACTIONS OF THE
ROYAL SOCIETY OF LITERATURE

NEW SERIES · VOLUME XXXV

EDITED BY

SHEILA BIRKENHEAD

F.R.S.L.

LONDON
OXFORD UNIVERSITY PRESS
NEW YORK   TORONTO
1969

*Oxford University Press, Ely House, London W. 1*

GLASGOW NEW YORK TORONTO MELBOURNE WELLINGTON
CAPE TOWN SALISBURY IBADAN NAIROBI LUSAKA ADDIS ABABA
BOMBAY CALCUTTA MADRAS KARACHI LAHORE DACCA
KUALA LUMPUR SINGAPORE HONG KONG TOKYO

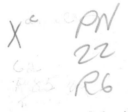

PRINTED IN GREAT BRITAIN

# CONTENTS

# INTRODUCTION

ONCE again the high quality and the variety in subject of the lectures delivered to the Royal Society of Literature during the year make it difficult for any editor to make a choice. Perhaps I may comment on those brought together in this anthology without adhering to the order in which they appear in the book.

Two of the papers concern our founder, King George IV. Miss Joanna Richardson, an expert in this period, considers him in the role of patron of literature. And a generous patron he was—presenting his father's library of more than 65,000 volumes to found the famous King's Library at the British Museum, supporting the Royal Literary Fund, expressing his pleasure that Sir Walter Scott's baronetcy was the first creation of his reign, and founding this Royal Society with a gift of eleven hundred guineas a year, which he continued until his death. From Mr. George Whalley we learn what the King's munificence meant to Coleridge, who was elected by the Council of the Society to be one of ten Royal Associates to receive an annual grant of one hundred guineas, their only duty being to read to the Society one paper a year on a subject of their own choice. This timely help eased Coleridge's financial anxieties until George IV's death, when his successor refused to continue the Royal bounty.

Other poets are discussed in this volume. Professor Blunden, in his study of Wordsworth's later poems, denies the widely held belief that the poet's genius waned in middle age, and suspects that Wordsworth was a more mysterious being than his friend Coleridge. Mr. Walter Allen gives us a vivid picture of Louis MacNeice from personal acquaintance—an aesthete and an intellectual, who was also a countryman and a lover of cricket and Rugby football—a man learned in classical and modern literature, who yet was deeply conscious of the senses and understood the life of action. Mr. Roy Fuller surveys the poetry of his time, from his discovery of Ezra Pound and Eliot when he was sixteen years old, to the 1960s, where he finds in the young a return to the conviction that the poet 'has some special message or warning about ordinary life'. I wish that we could have included in this volume, for the benefit of the general reader, some impression of the brilliant recital by Mr. Emlyn

Williams of Dylan Thomas's early writings, prose as well as poetry, which held Fellows and Members enthralled. But it was a 'performance', a *tour de force*, rather than a lecture, so that it does not fall within the scope of this anthology.

In *Writing on Art* Mr. John Pope-Hennessy considers the problem of transmitting what the writer has seen through the medium of the written word, a problem which was even more intractable before the coming of photography. He compares various writers on art, from Vasari to Berenson, and points out that the most moving prose may fail to convey the atmosphere or the content of a work of art as vividly as a less eloquent passage. Mr. Pope-Hennessy, from the depth of his own experience, emphasizes that those who are interested in art should, above all, be taught to look. We remember Ruskin's teaching and Charlotte Brontë's tribute to him, when she said that his book *Modern Painters* had given her a new sense—sight.

How the people of Florence rediscovered Greek and Roman literature; how these discoveries led for the first time in the Middle Ages to the study of secular history and the winning of civic liberties in ancient times; how this new knowledge affected their lives, and through them our own, is the subject of Mr. Vincent Cronin's engrossing essay on *The Classical Ideal in Florence*.

These discoveries led to the classical tradition which was for so long the mainstay of English education, and Professor Randolph Quirk, in his paper on *The Conception of Good Grammar*, analyses the many different meanings applied to the word 'grammar'. It is right and proper that a lecture on the bones of our language should be included in this collection.

What novelist had a better or more disciplined control of language than Jane Austen? And may her economical and accurate use of words have been due in part to the classical education which, with her brothers, she early imbibed from her father, who had been a Fellow of St. John's College and known at Oxford as 'the handsome proctor'? In Mr. Leslie Hartley's masterly essay on Jane Austen he analyses the element of sadness in her books and searches for a sense of approaching calamity. But many of his listeners must surely have been momentarily diverted from this original line of inquiry by the unexpected revelation of the lecturer in the rôle of 'Gunner Hartley'.

Another woman novelist, Maria Edgeworth, whose bicentenary we have been celebrating, is the subject of an essay by

Lord Evans, which should bring back many readers to this neglected writer. Her work was much admired by Scott and also by Ruskin, who used to read her books aloud to his guests. Lord Evans tells us how she lived at the heart of an enormous Irish family and how, in his opinion, all that is best in her work derives from Ireland. This Irish connection leads us to the paper on Jonathan Swift in which Mr. Michael Foot takes up the cudgels vigorously against Macaulay, Scott, and Dr. Johnson, and commends to political journalists Swift's dictum, which he has clearly taken to heart himself: 'Use the point of the pen, not the feather.'

We have read about George IV as a patron of literature, but it is interesting to remember that an equally good case can be made for him as a lover of music, architecture, silver or pictures. He would surely have approved of the diversity of subjects included in the lectures delivered this year to the Society which he founded.

SHEILA BIRKENHEAD

# KATJA REISSNER LECTURE

This lecture perpetuates the memory of Katja Reissner, musician and lover of literature, who died in December 1952. It was founded by her son, Alexander Reissner, a Member of this Society since 1946.

---

# LOUIS MACNEICE

*By* WALTER ALLEN, F.R.S.L.

(*Read 7 December 1967*)

*C. Day Lewis, C.B.E., C.Lit., D.Litt., F.R.S.L., in the Chair*

IT is not my aim this evening to attempt an act of criticism; to try and 'place', as they say, Louis MacNeice in the hierarchy of the English poets or to define and assess the nature of his contribution to poetry. That is a task that for me, I think, would be impossible. Many of his poems have become part of my being; and I find it very difficult to separate the poetry from the man whom I knew, liked, and admired for more than thirty years, a man so vivid that to be with him was to feel oneself enhanced. And having said that, I must rapidly add that I was not by any means one of MacNeice's closest friends. But there were periods, especially in the years immediately before the war, when he was teaching at Bedford College, when I spent a great deal in his company; and though I do not imagine I played a great part in his life, I know he played a great part in mine.

I met him first in what must have been the autumn term of 1930, when I was an undergraduate in Birmingham University and he, I suppose, an assistant lecturer in classics just down from Oxford. I was a student in his Latin class. It would be nice to say that this was one of the great formative experiences of my life; but it would not be true. The *de officiis* of Cicero is not a work for which I have ever felt any affection, and, as I remember, our boredom in construing it was matched only by Louis's apparent boredom in teaching it. What I also remember is the impression Louis made on me. No doubt I was prepared to be impressed anyway. He had already published a book of verse, *Blind Fireworks*, and that made him the first recognized poet—

guaranteed as it were by the fact of publication—that I had set eyes on. But there was much more to it than that. In those days the Faculty of Arts in Birmingham University was housed in a building in the centre of the city, the old Mason College, a Victorian Gothic structure that was one of the grimmest buildings ever built by man. It reeked, I recall, permanently of gas. In that atmosphere of gloom and grime, of dirty-brown pitch-pine boarding, perpetual artificial light, and the stink of gas from faulty pipes, in which, as Louis was to write later in *Autumn Journal*, 'the prison-like lecture room' resounded 'to Homer in a Dudley accent', he was a very exotic bird indeed. I wonder now which were the more surprised, he at the sight of us, lower middle class youths from Birmingham and the Black Country, or we at the sight of him. He was, as he remained all his life, an extraordinarily handsome man, but his handsomeness was of an unusual kind. He had the long Irish upper lip, but also the darkness of complexion, a certain Mediterranean quality, which I believe is usually referred back to the consequences of the Spanish sailors cast away on the west coast of Ireland after the scattering of the Armada. And then he was a dandy. In a B.B.C. programme about him after his death someone—I think it was Geoffrey Grigson—said he was an exquisite. If you can suppress the usual pejorative associations that go with it, the word is just. He wore the conventional uniform for young dons and students of the time, sports jacket and grey flannel trousers; but he wore them with a difference that one could only envy and not hope ever to match. The shirt, the tie, the handkerchief in the breast pocket—it was the choice of these in combination with the conventional garb that one could never hope to emulate; and it was the gradations and contrasts of colour that fascinated. 'Neat, but not gaudy'? No. Louis was always neat but he was often gaudy. This, I think, was part of his character, the outward expression, perhaps, of the violence that was never far below the surface and that sometimes erupted. But he could get away with gaudiness, partly because, if one calls him a dandy, an exquisite, he was a very complex dandy, a very complex exquisite. He was, plainly, in those days when I first saw him, an aesthete; but he was also in a curious way—and his manner of dress suggested it—something else one does not normally associate with aesthetes. There was also about him a strong tang of the countryman, the man of the open air. The writer of the obituary notice on him in the *Guardian* was reminded of an

Irish groom; and there was about him, I think, always the air of a man who was close to animals, to horses and dogs. This may be merely to say, though it was something it took me years to realize, that he was an Irishman. He was, then, an unusual kind of aesthete, and the unusualness lay in the fact that he was at the same time an unusual kind of hearty. He was a great watcher of games—the Tavern at Lords was one of the places one could normally expect to meet him—and a great player of games, of Rugger and tennis particularly. How good he was I do not know, but that he played with ferocity and to win I am perfectly certain.

He had, in other words, one foot always firmly set in the interests and activities of the common man; and this was part of his strength as a poet. I am guessing now, but I suspect that this was something he first discovered himself around 1935, which was the time when I really began to know him. Until then, as he tells us in his long fragment of autobiography, *The Strings are False*, a self-portrait which seems to me a speaking likeness of the MacNeice I knew, he had been living during his Birmingham years in a cocoon, one might almost say a fairyland or artificial paradise of domesticity. Then his marriage failed, he was alone, thrown on his own resources, and he discovered Birmingham, the industrial city and its people. It seems to have hit him like a revelation; it was almost, one guesses, like the sudden discovery of reality. You have to remember that, before this, he had scarcely known the industrial landscape, brought up as he was in the Ulster countryside, and then at school in England, at first near Sherborne and then at Marlborough, with Oxford after that. He was a man who lived in and through the senses and for whom the visible world existed in the most tangible and palpable way; and the shock of Birmingham, the sense of a new world quite different from and challenging anything he had experienced before, runs throughout his second volume of verse, *Poems*, which appeared in 1935. Some aspects of Birmingham he captured, I think, as no other writer has succeeded in doing.

Smoke from the train-gulf hid by hoardings blunders upward, the
    brake of cars
Pipe as the policeman pivoting round raises his flat hand, bars
With his figure of a monolith Pharaoh the queue of fidgety
    machines
(Chromium dogs on the bonnet, faces behind the triplex screens).
Behind him the streets run away between the proud glass of shops,

Cubical scent-bottles artificial legs arctic foxes and electric mops,
But beyond this centre the slumward vista thins like a diagram:
There, unvisited, are Vulcan's forges who doesn't care a tinker's
    damn.

Splayed outwards through the suburbs houses, houses for rest
Seducingly rigged by the builder, half-timbered houses with lips
    pressed
So tightly and eyes staring at the traffic through bleary haws
And only a six-inch gap of the racing earth in their concrete
    claws;
In these houses men as in a dream pursue the Platonic Forms
With wireless and cairn terriers and gadgets approximating to the
    fickle norms
And endeavour to find God and score one over the neighbour
By climbing tentatively upward on jerry-built beauty and sweated
    labour.

The lunch hour: the shops empty, shopgirls' faces relax
Diaphanous as green glass, empty as old almanacs
As incoherent with ticketed gewgaws tiered behind their heads
As the Burne-Jones windows in St. Philip's broken by crawling
    leads;
Insipid colour, patches of emotion, Saturday thrills
(This theatre is sprayed with 'June')—the gutter take our old
    playbills,
Next week-end it is likely in the heart's funfair we shall pull
Strong enough on the handle to get back our money; or at any
    rate it is possible.

On shining lines the trams like vast sarcophagi move
Into the sky, plum after sunset, merging to duck's egg, barred with
    mauve
Zepplin clouds, and Pentecost-like the cars' headlights bud
Out from sideroads and the traffic signals, crême-de-menthe or
    bull's blood,
Tell one to stop, the engine gently breathing, or to go on
To where like black pipes of organs in the frayed and fading zone
Of the West the factory chimneys on sullen sentry will all night
    wait
To call, in the harsh morning, sleep-stupid faces through the
    daily gate.

That is the poem called 'Birmingham'. It is essentially, I think,
a view from the outside: I do not think a native of the city
could have written it. When I first read it, it hit me like a
revelation. I was surprised into realization for the first time of
the dark, sullen power of the city. For MacNeice, it had, among
other things, an exotic splendour.

But Louis, I think, was on the outside wherever he was. All imaginative writers, or course, are on the outside; it is part of being a writer. But MacNeice's detachment—at times it could appear as aloofness—was more patent than that of most writers. No man, I think, had a greater appreciation of England; he had a wonderful zest both for London and for the English countryside, and he identified himself completely with England. But I doubt whether he thought of himself as an Englishman. He was, after all, Irish, and he became the more obstreperously Irish the drunker he got. But he was a pretty complex sort of Irishman. By birth he was an Ulsterman—his father was a clergyman who later became bishop—but he was in every way at odds with the Establishment of Ulster. Whether by temperament of circumstances, he was, I think, an outsider, very much the child among us taking notes. At the same time he was a gregarious man; but it was a strange kind of gregariousness. I have a fixed image of him in my mind. He is standing at the bar with a group of friends and colleagues in the Stag or the George or the Salisbury, fully in it but not quite of it: there is an expression on his face—everyone who knew him will I think remember this—almost of incredulity, the equivalent of a nudge inviting you to share his surprised delight at the oddity, the extravagance, the absurdity of human beings and their behaviour.

So far, all there seems to have emerged from this very subjective sketch is the impression of a man who united within himself opposites, who was defined, as it were, by opposites. The detached, aloof observer who, at the same time, might have applied to himself Browning's line, 'the need of a world of men for me'. And then the aesthete and intellectual—and I realize I have said nothing about his deep and wide learning in literature, classical and modern, in philosophy and psychology— who was equally the appreciator of the physical, the life of action, and the senses. Who, I am tempted to say, combined within himself and suggested in his very appearance and gesture the aristocrat and the peasant. This dichotomy in him comes out strongly in his poetry and formed indeed the basis of his view of the things. It is magically expressed in one of the best of his early poems, 'Snow':

The room was suddenly rich and the great bay-window was
Spawning snow and pink roses against it
Soundlessly collateral and incompatible:
World is suddener than we fancy it.

World is crazier and more of it than we think,
Incorrigibly plural. I peel and portion
A tangerine and spit the pips and feel
The drunkenness of things being various.

And the fire flames with a bubbling sound for world
Is more spiteful and gay than one supposes—
On the tongue on the eyes on the ears in the palms of one's hands—
There is more glass than between the snow and the huge roses.

It is at the heart, too, of that extraordinarily powerful poem 'An Eclogue for Christmas', which is really a dialogue between the two sides of him, the aesthete, the sophisticated townee, on the one hand, the countryman, the man of the open air, on the other. It begins, you will remember:

A. I meet you in an evil time.
B.                          The evil bells
   Put out our heads, I think, the thought of everything else.
A. The jaded calendar revolves,
   Its nuts need oil, carbon chokes the valves,
   The excess sugar of a diabetic culture
   Rotting the nerve of life and literature;
   Therefore when we bring out the old tinsel and frills
   To announce that Christ is born among the barbarous hills
   I turn to you whom a morose routine
   Saves from the mad vertigo of being what has been.
B. Analogue of me, you are wrong to turn on me,
   My country will not yield you any sanctuary,
   There is no pinpoint in any of the ordnance maps
   To save you when your towns and town-bred thoughts collapse,
   It is better to die *in situ* as I shall,
   One place is as bad as another. Go back where your instincts
     call
   And listen to the crying of the town-cats and the taxis again,
   Or wind your gramophone and eavesdrop on great men.

And here are the last lines.

A. I will gorge myself to satiety with the oddities
   Of every artiste, official or amateur,
   Who has pleased me in my rôle of hero-worshipper
   Who has pleased me in my rôle of individual man—
B. Let us lie once more, say 'What we think, we can'
   The old idealist lie—
A.                       And for me before I die
   Let me go the round of garish glare—
B.                                   And on the bare and high
   Places of England, the Wiltshire Downs and the Long Mynd

Let the balls of my feet bounce on the turf, my face burn in the
wind
My eyelashes stinging in the wind, and the sheep like grey
stones
Humble my human pretensions—
A.                      Let the saxophones and the xylophones
And the cult of every technical excellence, the miles of canvas
in the galleries
And the canvas of the rich man's yacht snapping and tacking
on the seas
And the perfection of a grilled steak—
B.                      Let all these so ephemeral things
Be somehow permanent like the swallow's tangent wings:
Goodbye to you, this day remember is Christmas, this morn
They say, interpret it your own way, Christ is born.

In these days MacNeice is almost inevitably tagged with the
label 'Thirties poet'. It is a fate that has befallen almost all the
English writers, the poets particularly, who made their first
reputations in the thirties; and it can obviously be both silly
and unfair. He is seen in other words as one of the four legs of the
monster Roy Campbell created in the figure of MacSpaundey,
the other legs being, of course, yourself, Mr. Chairman, W. II.
Auden, and Stephen Spender. But at the time itself, to those
of who were reading the works of these poets as they appeared,
MacNeice seemed not to belong to them at all but to stand
significantly apart. 'An Eclogue for Christmas' contains these
two lines:

> We shall go down like palaeolithic man
> Before some new Ice Age or Genghiz Khan.

If you think of Thirties poetry as being largely politically
oriented, which is of course grossly to over-simplify, then those
lines will seem very uncharacteristic, written as they were at
much the same time as Wystan Auden was praying for 'new
styles of architecture, / a change of heart', and Stephen Spender
was celebrating the future state in such lines as:

> Death is another milestone on their way.
> With laughter on their lips and with winds blowing round them
> They speak simply
> Of how this one excelled all others in making driving belts.

And when one read MacNeice's poem, 'The Individualist
Speaks', with its last line, '—But I will escape, with my dog, on
the far side of the Fair', it was difficult to avoid reading into it
a repudiation of mass movements in politics whether of the

Left or the Right. Indeed, there runs through the poems he wrote in the thirties a sense of foreboding, of impending doom for himself and for people like him; as in this poem, 'Turf-stacks'.

> Among these turf-stacks graze no iron horses
> Such as stalk, such as champ in towns and the soul of crowds,
> Here is no mass-production of neat thoughts
> No canvas shrouds for the mind nor any black hearses:
> The peasant shambles on his boots like hooves
> Without thinking at all or wanting to run in grooves.
>
> But those who lack the peasant's conspirators,
> The tawny mountain, the unregarded buttress,
> Will feel the need of a fortress against ideas and against the
> Shuddering insidious shock of the theory-vendors,
> The little sardine men crammed in a monster toy
> Who tilt their aggregate beast against our crumbling Troy.
>
> For we are obsolete who like the lesser things
> Who play in corners with looking-glasses and beads;
> It is better we should go quickly, go into Asia
> Or any other tunnel where the world recedes,
> Or turn blind wantons like the gulls who scream
> And rip the edge off any ideal or dream.

This is not to deny at all that his political sympathies were towards the Left, but he was much less committed politically than some other poets of the period. Yet in spite of this, perhaps even because of it, he seems to me essentially a Thirties poet and to have remained one. He did not have to repudiate his early work as Auden—to my regret—has felt it necessary to repudiate so much of his. His underwent no conversions; there are no dramatic changes in the nature of his poetry or in the preoccupations that inform it, as, again, there have been in Auden's. Indeed, there is no obvious development in his poetry. The verses in his second volume, *Poems*, which made his reputation, are as good as anything he ever wrote; what he did in the thirty years that followed was to go on writing poems that were as good; but already, in that early volume, he was the master of his medium, and, I believe, a totally original poet.

And the thirties, I think, was the right period for him to have emerged in, and better than anyone else, it seems to me, he sums up its poetic virtues. In so far as it can be seen as a self-contained period—and, in literature, it was more self-contained than decades normally are—it was characterized in poetry by a strong reaction against symbolism, against private poetry, in opposition to which it set up the notion of public poetry, public in the sense that it should be accessible to all men and women of goodwill. It could be topical, light, slangy, and its imagery was to be derived as required from the furnishings of the world of the common man. The word 'journalistic' as applied to poetry suddenly took on connotations of praise. The poets of the time often fell far short, of course, of their ambitions in these respects; but they are more successful, it seems to me, than they are sometimes given credit for. Today we find their aims embodied in the poetry of, for instance, Philip Larkin and Kingsley Amis; and to turn to much more popular poets, you can spot the influence of Auden in some of the lyrics of the Beatles. They were attempting, in fact, the kind of poetry J. M. Synge had in mind, when he wrote:

I have often thought that at the side of poetic diction, which everyone condemns, modern verse uses a great deal of poetic material, using poetic in the same special sense. The poetry of exaltation will always be the highest, but when men lose their poetic feeling for ordinary life, and cannot write poetry of ordinary things, their exalted poetry is likely to lose its strength of exaltation, in the way men cease to build beautiful churches when they have lost happiness in building shops. Many of the older poets, such as Villon and Herrick and Burns, used the whole of their personal life as their material, and the verse written in this way was read by strong men, and thieves, and deacons, not by little cliques alone.

Significantly, MacNeice quotes that passage in his book *Modern Poetry*, and in the last chapter he produces a paraphrase of it in terms of himself.

My own prejudice [he writes] is in favour of poets whose worlds are not too esoteric. I would have a poet able-bodied, fond of talking, a reader of the newspapers, capable of pity and laughter, informed in economics, appreciative of women, involved in personal relationships, susceptible to physical impressions.

It would be easy to draw up a long list of poets, some of them among the greatest, who would fall lamentably short of MacNeice's requirements; but the important point is that, when all allowances have been made for the especial circumstances of the time at which it was written—1938—it remains a very adequate description of MacNeice himself and very well indicates the kind of life, the world if you like, you find in his poetry. His was not the poetry of exaltation, anything but. It is often a pyrotechnic display of hard, bright, dazzling images, of unexpected rhymes unexpectedly placed; it uses echoes of nursery rhymes and takes in slang and cliché—in homage to which he wrote a memorable poem; it is often highly topical. And always MacNeice makes words dance to his own tune; and one of the pleasures I find in his poetry is the sense of the pleasure Mac-Neice himself got in writing it, the delight in his own virtuosity, his sheer technical expertise. It is a highly idiosyncratic poetry which is always the vehicle of highly idiosyncratic personal comment, allied often to the essay, even to the newspaper columnist's article. There are, I feel, though I speak without knowledge, affinities with Horace. It may not be always apparent on the surface. In England Horace is traditionally turned into a clubman, whereas Louis was a pubman, a very different animal. But the beautiful translations he made from Horace show the feeling he had for him; and I think the affinity goes further than this.

I find it difficult simply because there are so many poems to choose from, to illustrate MacNeice as the poet of personal comment. But every fine Sunday morning, when I look down from my upper window on to the street, this poem comes into my mind:

> Down the road someone is practising scales,
> The notes like little fishes vanish with a wink of tails,
> Man's heart expands to tinker with his car
> For this is Sunday morning, Fate's great bazaar;
> Regard these means as ends, concentrate on this Now,
> And you may grow to music or drive beyond Hindhead anyhow,
> Take corners on two wheels until you go so fast
> That you can clutch a fringe or two of the windy past,
> That you can abstract this day and make it to the week of time
> A small eternity, a sonnet self-contained in rhyme.
>
> But listen, up the road, something gulps, the church spire
> Opens its eight bells out, skulls' mouths which will not tire
> To tell how there is no music or movement which secures
> Escape from the weekday time. Which deadens and endures.

That poem is in fact called 'Sunday Morning'. He had an unerring sense of the moment and of the time of which the separate moment is a part; a wonderful sense, too, of the moment that transcends time; as in this poem, 'Meeting Point', in my view one of the best love poems of our age.

> Time was away and somewhere else,
> There were two glasses and two chairs
> And two people with the one pulse
> (Somebody stopped the moving stairs):
> Time was away and somewhere else.

And they were neither up nor down;
The stream's music did not stop
Flowing through heather, limpid brown,
Although they sat in a coffee shop
And they were neither up nor down.

The bell was silent in the air
Holding its inverted poise—
Between the clang and clang a flower,
A brazen calyx of no noise:
The bell was silent in the air.

The camels crossed the miles of sand
That stretched around the cups and plates:
The desert was their own, they planned
To portion out the stars and dates:
The camels crossed the miles of sand.

Time was away and somewhere else.
The waiter did not come, the clock
Forgot them and the radio waltz
Came out like water from a rock:
Time was away and somewhere else.

Her fingers flicked away the ash
That bloomed again in tropic trees:
Not caring if the markets crash
When they had forests such as these,
Her fingers flicked away the ash.

God or whatever means the Good
Be praised that time can stop like this,
That what the heart has understood
Can verify in the body's peace
God or whatever means the Good.

Time was away and she was here
And life no longer what it was,
The bell was silent in the air
And all the room one glow because
Time was away and she was here.

He had a wonderful feeling, too, for the climate, the defining
smell, of a specific time. I suppose the obvious example of this is
what is perhaps his most famous poem, 'Bagpipe Music', which
is a triumph of virtuosity and energy, a comic poem with
sinister undertones that captures completely, it seems to me,
the hopelessness and helplessness of the thirties as manifested
in one particular region.

It's no go the merrygoround, it's no go the rickshaw,
All we want is a limousine and a ticket for the peepshow.
Their knickers are made of crêpe-de-chine, their shoes are made of
    python,
Their halls are lined with tiger rugs and their walls with heads of
    bison.

John MacDonald found a corpse, put it under the sofa,
Waited till it came to life and hit it with a poker,
Sold its eyes for souvenirs, sold its blood for whisky,
Kept its bones for dumb-bells to use when he was fifty.

It's no go the Yogi-Man, it's no go Blavatsky,
All we want is a bank balance and a bit of skirt in a taxi.

Annie MacDougall went to milk, caught her foot in the heather,
Woke to hear a dance record playing of Old Vienna.
It's no go your maidenheads, it's no go your culture,
All we want is a Dunlop tyre and the devil mend the puncture.

The Laird o' Phelps spent Hogmanay declaring he was sober,
Counted his feet to prove the fact and found he had one foot over.
Mrs. Carmichael had her fifth, looked at the job with repulsion,
Said to the midwife 'Take it away; I'm through with over-
    production'.

It's no go the gossip column, it's no go the ceilidh,
All we want is a mother's help and a sugar-stick for the baby.

Willy Murray cut his thumb, couldn't count the damage,
Took the hide of an Ayrshire cow and used it for a bandage.
His brother caught three hundred cran when the seas were lavish,
Threw the bleeders back in the sea and went upon the parish.

It's no go the Herring Board, it' no go the Bible,
All we want is a packet of fags when our hands are idle.

It's no go the picture palace, it's no go the stadium,
It's no go the country cot with a pot of pink geraniums,
It's no go the Government grants, it's no go the elections,
Sit on your arse for fifty years and hang your hat on a pension.

It's no go my honey love, it's no go my poppet;
Work your hands from day to day, the winds will blow the profit.
The glass is falling hour by hour, the glass will fall for ever,
But if you break the bloody glass you won't hold up the weather.

His most sustained rendering of a specific time is the long
sequence—there are ninety-six pages of it—*Autumn Journal*,
which appeared in 1939. By any standard this seems to me a
remarkable achievement, probably his greatest. It is, as the

title says, a journal, a journal written in verse from August 1938 to the following New Year. It is, in other words, a fragment of autobiography that takes in Munich and the aftermath of Munich; it is the product of immediate experience at a time when the experience itself was forcing many of us, Louis certainly, to question our previous lives and all we had taken for granted in the light of imminent war and possible death. You could say *Autumn Journal* is journalistic. So it is; and that is part of its value. One thing I am sure of, and that is that it will be read for as long as anyone is interested in the last war and the months immediately before it. If anyone wants to know what it was like to be a young, very intelligent, sensitive man in the autumn of 1938, this is the book to read. It is a unique document. That, I am aware, does not make it a good poem; but I believe it is also just that, a good poem, one quite unlike any other in the language. It is a tremendous feat of poetic tightrope walk, for it is poetry almost at the level of conversation; but since it *is* poetry it is more exact than conversation can ever be, and is both more economical and more evocative than prose. In it, MacNeice records the times as he felt them, himself and examines his life, past and present, as it revealed itself to him in the dramatically different circumstances of those times. It becomes a summary of his life up to the moment of the poem's end. To quote a single line or even a few lines would be to show nothing of the poem's quality, for the unit of the poem is not the line but something much more like the paragraph as we know it in prose. It has to be quoted *in extenso* if its quality is to be seen, and the passage I have chosen to read is the ninth section, written early in October with the Munich crisis over and MacNeice about to return to his job as Lecturer in Greek at Bedford College.

## IX

Now we are back to normal, now the mind is
    Back to the even tenor of the usual day
Skidding no longer across the uneasy camber
    Of the nightmare way.
*We* are safe though others have crashed the railings
    Over the river ravine; their wheel-tracks carve the bank
But after the event all we can do is argue
    And count the widening ripples where they sank.
October comes with rain whipping around the ankles
    In waves of white at night

And filling the raw clay trenches (the parks of London
    Are a nasty sight).
In a week I return to work, lecturing, coaching,
    As impresario of the Ancient Greeks
Who wore the chiton and lived on fish and olives
    And talked philosophy or smut in cliques;
Who believed in youth and did not gloze the unpleasant
    Consequences of age;
What is life, one said, or what is pleasant
    Once you have turned the page
Of love? The days grow worse, the dice are loaded
    Against the living man who pays in tears for breath;
Never to be born was the best, call no man happy
    This side death.
Conscious—long before Engels—of necessity
    And therein free
They plotted out their life with truism and humour
    Between the jealous heaven and the callous sea.
And Pindar sang the garland of wild olive
    And Alcibiades lived from hand to mouth
Double-crossing Athens, Persia, Sparta,
    And many died in the city of plague, and many of drouth
In Sicilian quarries, and many by the spear and arrow
    And many more who told their lies too late
Caught in the eternal factions and reactions
    Of the city-state.
And free speech shivered on the pikes of Macedonia
    And later on the swords of Rome
And Athens became a mere university city
    And the goddess born of the foam
Became the kept hetaera, heroine of Menander,
    And the philosopher narrowed his focus, confined
His efforts to putting his own soul in order
    And keeping a quiet mind.
And for a thousand years they went on talking,
    Making such apt remarks,
A race no longer of heroes but of professors
    And crooked business men and secretaries and clerks
Who turned out dapper little elegiac verses
    On the ironies of fate, the transience of all
Affections, carefully shunning an over-statement
    But working the dying fall.
The Glory that was Greece: put it in a syllabus, grade it
    Page by page
To train the mind or even to point a moral
    For the present age:

Models of logic and lucidity, dignity, sanity,
   The golden mean between opposing ills
Though there were exceptions of course but only exceptions—
   The bloody Bacchanals on the Thracian hills.
So the humanist in his room with Jacobean panels
   Chewing his pipe and looking on a lazy quad
Chops the Ancient World to turn a sermon
   To the greater glory of God.
But I can do nothing so useful or so simple;
   These dead are dead
And when I should remember the paragons of Hellas
   I think instead
Of the crooks, the adventurers, the opportunists,
   The careless athletes and the fancy boys,
The hair-splitters, the pedants, the hard-boiled sceptics
   And the Agora and the noise
Of the demagogues and the quacks; and the women pouring
   Libations over graves
And the trimmers at Delphi and the dummies at Sparta and lastly
   I think of the slaves.
And how one can imagine oneself among them
   I do not know;
It was all so unimaginably different
   And all so long ago.

MacNeice was to return to the mode of *Autumn Journal* sixteen years later in *Autumn Sequel* but with nothing like the success of the earlier poem, partly, perhaps, because the personal element in it—*Autumn Sequel* is a celebration of friendship, a portrait gallery almost of his friends—is insufficiently curbed by the sense of a hard refractory world outside. Which is perhaps only another way of saying that it is too self-indulgent. For I think it has to be admitted that MacNeice was at times the victim of his facility, his dazzling technical skill, and when the pressure behind his work was low, as I feel it is in *Autumn Sequel*, one realizes that dazzle alone is not enough. When the pressure was low what resulted was something like self-parody, which must be the intermittent fate of every strongly idiosyncratic writer. One thinks of Faulkner or Graham Greene, for instance. But it seems to me that MacNeice did strike a bad patch in the late 1940s and the 1950s. Times had changed and notions of poetry had changed; and he had not changed with them. Indeed, there was a point when younger poets and critics seemed to have written him off.

For this apparent falling off in his powers it was fashionable to blame his long years of work as a feature-writer at the B.B.C.

Well, he had his living to earn, and he found the work and the company congenial, more congenial, I am pretty sure, than the obvious alternative, which was university teaching. And the work he wrote for the B.B.C. was a completely legitimate extension of the function of poetry as he understood it. He took to writing for radio and to production too—he was a very brilliant producer—like a duck to water. One looks back to perhaps the first half of his years in radio as to the high peak of sound broadcasting, when the radio feature became an art, an ephemeral art admittedly but still an art. MacNeice, of course, was not alone in making radio an art; he was one among many; but he did give it an elegance, a sense of style, a vividness, and a verbal distinction that was his own and essentially that of his poems.

In any event, it is a rash act to write off any poet, or novelist for that matter, so long as he is still alive; and in MacNeice's case there was in the last years of his life a new outburst of creative energy that produced poems certainly as fine as any he had written before. This is particularly true of the poems in the collection *The Burning Perch*, which appeared within a matter of weeks after his unexpected death in September 1963. Posthumous volumes, especially when they appear so quickly after a poet's death, are an open invitation to sentimentality: it is almost impossible not to read them differently from the way in which we read the work of the man while alive; and it would be easy to read into the poems of *The Burning Perch* premonitions of the poet's death. MacNeice himself said that he had been 'taken aback', while preparing the volume for the press, 'by the high proportion of sombre pieces, ranging from bleak observations to thumbnail nightmares'. He had, of course, always been aware of the dark underside of things, of the terror of life, and mortality; they are there in his work from the beginning. He was, I think, an unillusioned, stoic humanist very much in the tradition of E. M. Forster; and like Forster's Mrs. Moore, he had heard the 'oum-boum' of the echo in the Marabar Caves. And certainly *The Burning Perch* is the most sombre of his collections: 'bleak observations', 'thumbnail nightmares'—the descriptions are accurate. All the same, the sombreness is lit up by the energy of the wit and a grim, sardonic, almost contemptuous gaiety. They are the poems, I feel, of a man who knows the worst and is not intimidated, the poetic equivalents of the smile, almost the snarl of derision, one had sometimes seen on Louis's face in life.

All along, I have been bothered by problems of choice of poems to illustrate this talk with, and it is still with me now. But here to end with, is a poem from *The Burning Perch*, 'The Introduction'; perhaps MacNeice's final statement on the incongruity of things.

> They were introduced in a grave glade
> And she frightened him because she was young
> And thus too late. Crawly crawly
> Went the twigs above their heads and beneath
> The grass beneath their feet the larvae
> Split themselves laughing. Crawly crawly
> Went the cloud above the treetops reaching
> For a sun that lacked the nerve to set
> And he frightened her because he was old
> And thus too early. Crawly crawly
> Went the string quartet that was tuning up
> In the back of the mind. You two should have met
> Long since, he said, or else not now.
> The string quartet in the back of the mind
> Was all tuned up with nowhere to go.
> They were introduced in a green grave.

# TREDEGAR MEMORIAL LECTURE

This lecture perpetuates the memory of the first
Viscount Tredegar. It was founded in 1935 by his
son, a Fellow of this Society from 1928 until 1949.

# WORDSWORTH'S LATER POEMS

*By* EDMUND BLUNDEN, C.B.E., M.C., C.LIT., LITT.D., F.R.S.L.

*(Read 24 March 1966)*

*The Lord Butler, C.H., P.C., in the Chair*

IT may be due to an early habit of reading the contents of a
favourite book of poems all through, partly because we did not
seem to possess these in vast numbers, that I never accepted as
law the frequent assertion concerning Wordsworth's later poems.
These, I was told, were hardly worth attention, and in his
fifties or thereabouts his genius sank and his poetic light grew
dull and monotonous. But was it not rather the case, I would
ask myself, that Wordsworth had felt as years went on a
possibility of new things to say in verse, new needs on the part
of his readers, and perhaps a willingness to hear other tones and
harmonies than had so long been assumed as the only genuine
poetical communication?

Accordingly I made a point of listing some of Wordsworth's
less-noticed poems belonging to his supposed period of lack of
appeal as I persuaded myself that they appealed to me; and
I can still read them with early veneration and acceptance.
There is one of these pieces which, if my surmise is right, has of
late been honoured with a kind of promotion and admission
'to the equal sky', and which may be pointed out at once as a
poem of this remarkable poet's age, distinct in its style and
voice from that he might have been expected to produce. It is
entitled—this is of course Wordsworthian enough whether of
one date or another—'Extempore Effusion upon the Death of
James Hogg'. It is a threnody, such as Shakespeare might have
intoned; the date of composition was 1835, and though perhaps
the disappearance of Hogg from the literary world might not
have caused Wordsworth the most afflicting thoughts yet there

was much that did at the time. Here too I am stirred by the
fact that after all the oldest reader of these inspired poets can
never be sure what will come from them 'in dream'. We may
find prose records of a lesser magnanimity towards Coleridge
on Wordsworth's part than we find it pleasant to reflect upon.
But in the 'Extempore Effusion' we hear the voice of the bard
as nobly as in the poetry of Blake:

> Nor has the rolling year twice measured,
> From sign to sign, its steadfast course,
> Since every mortal power of Coleridge
> Was frozen at its marvellous source;
>
> The rapt one, of the godlike forehead,
> The heaven-eyed creature sleeps in earth;
> And Lamb, the frolic and the gentle,
> Has vanished from his lonely hearth.
>
> Like clouds that rake the mountain-summits,
> Or waves that own no curbing hand,
> How fast has brother followed brother,
> From sunshine to the sunless land.

In 1830 we find Wordsworth writing in ordinary rhymed
stanzas, such as the eighteenth-century clergyman would have
been thoroughly happy to achieve, a plain lyric of over twenty
lines—but the subject is 'Presentiments'. Why should this
poetical man, supposed to occupy himself with the normal
occurrences of life in the Lake District, suddenly come out with
these antique fashioned stanzas or such an unusual poetic
theme? What indeed does Wordsworth mean all through his
poem on the elusive subject, 'Presentiments'? He was ever a
strange being, and this matter was included in the sheep-fold
of strange William. May I offer a comment or two on 'Presentiments' and the author? He has at any rate not changed
observably in taking his subject closely from himself. As for
these 'Presentiments', he goes straight ahead:

> The tear whose source I could not guess,
> The deep sigh that seemed fatherless,
>     Were mine in early days;
> And now, unforced by time to part
> With fancy, I obey my heart,
>     And venture on your praise.

Presently the poetry over floods the contemplations, and dare
I hold that a mystery of its own period, of its own discovery
comes into this?

> But who can fathom your intents,
> Number their signs or instruments?
>    A rainbow, a sunbeam,
> A subtle smell that Spring unbinds,
> Dead pause abrupt of midnight winds,
>    An echo, or a dream.

These peculiar things 'presentiments' in a later stanza do not show Mr. Wordsworth pouring out the sherry or praising the daffodils.

> Ye daunt the proud array of war,
> Pervade the lonely ocean far
>    As sail hath been unfurled;
> For dancers in the festive hall
> What ghastly partners hath your call
>    Fetched from the shadowy world.

There is a Wordsworthian shadowy world now, without any praise or blame to Coleridge floating about it.

> 'Tis said that warnings ye dispense,
> Emboldened by a keener sense;
>    That men have lived, for whom,
> With dread precision, ye made clear
> The hour that in a distant year
>    Should knell them to the tomb.

The magnificent if not at every point interesting Ode 'On the Power of Sound' was composed by Wordsworth in 1828, and if I venture to call it in his later manner, I am sure that I claim no discovery about him or his meditations on poetry. Those who look at his prefixed 'Argument' will delight in his opening words, 'The Ear addressed'—to proceed, 'as occupied by a spiritual functionary, in communion with sounds, individual or combined in studied harmony'. And so he continues. This time the Lake Poet is curiously melodramatic. After a passage which may have been written with Keats in mind and a miscellany of Fauns and Satyrs and Bacchanalian revellers he suddenly calls for law and order of a sort:

> To life, to *life* give back thine ear;
> Ye who are longing to be rid
> Of fable, though to truth subservient, hear
> The little sprinkling of cold earth that fell
> Echoed from the coffin-lid;
> The convict's summons in the steeple's knell;
> 'The vain distress-gun,' from a leeward shore,
> Repeated—heard, and heard no more!

It has sometimes haunted my thought that Wordsworth was a more mysterious being than his friend Coleridge, but then he was apt to announce and throw what light he could on that something which is called the vision or perhaps the visionary splendour. His interest in the world develops as his life advances. Coleridge in later years has a reverie of being transferred with 'The Delinquent Travellers' whom he sees on the not too dismal ship, while notions of the world to be play over his mind; and Wordsworth, no longer with Coleridge as once he would have been, increases constantly in his conscience of things that may, indeed almost must, accompany humanity through the new century he so strangely enters and surveys.

Two poems written by Wordsworth in March 1833 have never made a clear impression on me, though the title of the first seems to usher in a reasonably simple work. It is 'To ———, Upon the Birth of her First-Born Child, March 1833'. It is of the benevolent and hopeful strain which would be expected on such an occasion, though there is an anxiety to be observed in the opening lines: perhaps the young mother was prepared for any sort of meditation from the old prophetic poet.

> Like a shipwrecked Sailor tost
> By rough waves on a perilous coast,
> Lies the Babe, in helplessness
> And in tenderest nakedness,
> Flung by labouring Nature forth
> Upon the mercies of the earth.
> Can its eyes beseech?—no more
> Than the hands are free to implore;
> Voice but serves for one brief cry;
> Plaint was it? or prophecy
> Of sorrow that will surely come?
> Omen of man's grievous doom!

Having at any rate achieved in eighty lines blessings and sacred predictions with 'starry promises' and a fairly confident forecast of 'serene weather', Wordsworth produces a much longer poem called 'The Warning. A Sequel to the Foregoing'. I can hardly believe that the young mother made her way through all this or if she did was able to be sure of the meaning. In the earlier movements Wordsworth appears to be imagining and depicting general rejoicings at the news of the 'unconscious Babe' acclaimed with love and tradition but moves from his agreeable celebration towards a difficult history of national anxieties—

And saw, thereafter, on the soil of France
Rash Polity begin her maniac dance,
Foundations broken up, the deeps run wild . . .

He then broods over political dangers, demands, misguidings, apparently hanging over the future not of France but of Britain, and if the sleeping mother wakes and has the power of reading him she must be bewildered that the seemingly calm Nature poet can have such fears invading his mood of delight at sight of the 'dear Babe'. Again the strangeness which is also in the subtle nature of Wordsworth perplexes me as the song of natural welcome alters into a mysterious warning, as he has surprised us in his additional title. He is thinking grimly, and though I pass his vision of 'blood-stained hands in frenzy' I still bring in the unexpected Wordsworth of the later years.

Thus, ungrateful Nation!
If thou persist, and scorning moderation,
Spread for thyself the snares of tribulation,
Whom, then, shall meekness guard? What saving skill
Lie in forbearance, strength in standing still?
—Soon shall the widow (for the speed of Time
Nought equals when the hours are winged with crime)
Widow, or wife, implore on tremulous knee,
From him who judged her lord, a like decree;
The skies will weep o'er old men desolate;
Ye little ones! Earth shudders at your fate,
Outcasts and homeless orphans—

And so he seems to be looking into the menacing future, nearly two centuries ahead, with as great an anguish as could be felt over all the pangs of mankind—but it is a blessing that he will not word all his visions any further, and suddenly seems to be reminded that on the occasion of these songs he was really due to salute a mother and a new-born baby with music and no doubt pretty presents.

Then he grows calm and almost clerical; but he has kept these rather terrifying verses no matter who may have wished he was still writing in the style which had pleased so many peaceful spirits long before.

Some may have longed that instead of the 'Warning', his eulogy of the Cuckoo Clock had been brought forward once more to illustrate Wordsworth's poetry of later years, and it need not only have been for entertainment by the way; but it seems to me that his genius even in his later discoveries of himself is not only there in his book for the entertainment he sometimes gave without knowing.

# THE CLASSICAL IDEAL IN FLORENCE

*By* VINCENT CRONIN, F.R.S.L.

*(Read 16 March 1967)*

*John Pope-Hennessy, C.B.E., F.B.A., F.S.A., F.R.S.L., in the Chair*

THIS evening I want to try to do three closely related things: describe how the Florentines discovered Greek and Roman literature, see what effect that discovery had on their lives and works, and thirdly, assess the relevance their enthronement of the classical ideal has for us today.

I would like to start if I may by refreshing your minds about Florence in the year 1390. It is more a market-town than a city — you can walk right across it in 25 minutes. You notice two prominent landmarks: the bristling tower of the Palazzo Vecchio and Giotto's rose and white marble belfry—the dome has not yet been built. The Baptistery is there, and Santa Maria Novella and Santa Croce. The Arno is crossed by four bridges. On one of them, the Ponte Vecchio, stand the butchers' shops— an advanced measure of hygiene of which the Florentines are rather proud. The population numbers about 50,000 and the well-to-do among them make their money from banking and textiles. Some of the men have hands violet or red from dyeing the thick Cotswold wool. They export textiles mainly to the East—scarlet and saffron and azure blue: Florence can be said to live by colour. The town has a republican constitution, almost unique at that time, and painfully evolved after the Dark Ages to meet the needs of a trading community. About 6,000 men are citizens, with the right to vote their own laws and fill the offices of government. There are no lords here, no one bows and scrapes, and people call one another by first names.

The town's immediate past has been rather gloomy. The Black Death killed off two out of three people, then came a financial crash. The town has produced three great men, Giotto, Dante, and Petrarch, but they were little appreciated by their compatriots and did their best work outside Florence. There is a university college, but it is starved of funds, and at the moment shut down. The people are hard-working, thrifty, terse, pungent, more religious than most. But Padua, with its medical school and Aristotelian experts, Bologna with its law faculty. Venice with its Eastern links—these in 1390 are the favourites for the steeplechase of history. Florence is an outsider.

Perhaps the most interesting man in the town at this time was Coluccio Salutati. He was then aged 60, burly, with a big scholar's head and a slight stoop. The son of a soldier, he had trained as a notary and for fifteen years now had been chancellor, top post in the civil service. When he married he ordered 3,000 oranges for the wedding feast—oranges were a luxury then—which points to a generous nature, for he was not rich. As chancellor he got the equivalent of £300 a year, but out of this he managed to build up a good library and indulge his tastes as a scholar. He was a humble man and disliked being addressed as *dominus*, for that, he said, implied that his correspondent was a slave.

Scholars in the past—even Petrarch—had been clerics. The important thing about Coluccio is that he was a layman. So his interests were new. Instead of getting excited about St. Jerome on the penitential psalms, Coluccio wanted to know how men in the past had been governed and taxed, how they voted laws and defended their frontiers—and by the past he meant the remote classical past, for this was the only period before his own century about which records remained. The answer to these questions was very difficult to find, for the classical past was partly a lost book, partly a closed one. By this I mean that Greek literature and history were wholly unknown in Florence, and Roman literature, save for a few works, was closed by the Church. The notable exceptions were Virgil's *Aeneid*, and Ovid's poetry, though this was distorted to yield an edifying meaning: the licentious *Ars Amoris* was deemed a manual of spiritual love, a guide for the soul seeking God. Some Livy was known and those parts of Cicero in harmony with Christianity. There were also dozens of tags and quotations and little vignettes like Diogenes in his barrel, symbolizing poverty— good sound stuff as far, that is, as pagans could be good. But it was impossible with the information available to get to know the Greeks and Romans as living people, to analyse their values or their motives. These were hidden, and the most conscientious churchmen were determined that they should remain hidden. The leading Dominican in Florence—Giovanni Dominici—said rather than Italian bambini should be brought up on Terence and pagan literature generally, he would prefer a new Pharaoh to arise and butcher the lot. And he meant it.

Coluccio disagreed. Others had felt disagreement before, but Coluccio, as I have said, was a soldier's son and he decided to do something about it. Coluccio argued in considerable detail why he and others should read pagan books, and we happen to have his arguments collected by Dominici in a work called *Lucula Noctis, The Fire-fly*. It was really the first time a Christian layman had got to his feet and demanded the right to study not just the facts of faith—if you see what I mean—but facts as such. His arguments now seem fairly obvious but they are worth looking at in some detail, because unless he had put them forward and unless they had finally prevailed, there would have been no such thing as the study of literature, no society of literature, and we should not be here tonight.

Coluccio started by saying that truth, by whomsoever it is stated, comes ultimately from God, and this holds of literature just as much as of arithmetic and music. The latter, being approved school subjects, were allowed to draw on Greek and Roman sources, so why not literature? A second point made by Coluccio was that in earlier days the holiest and most useful churchmen, such as Jerome and Augustine, had been steeped in the classics, indeed Augustine had been converted partly by reading Cicero's *Hortensius*. This, however, was not very convincing because there is a famous passage in Jerome where Christ appears to him in the desert and asks whether he is a Christian. Jerome replies that he is. No, says Christ, you are a Ciceronian. And after that Jerome stops reading the classics.

Coluccio went on to say that the study of literature is a perfectly natural desire, and grace should perfect not destroy nature. This seems to me a stronger argument than his next one: that literature is conducive to right living, since the philosophy enshrined in it is an ally of the moral life. Shades of James Bond and Oswald! Coluccio has one other argument— apparently unimportant, but as we shall see later, it was to prove the most effective—and it was an argument drawn from his own experience as chancellor. Studying literature and history, he said, would provide him and other politicians with a fund of political wisdom—it would help them to run their cities better. This appeal to practical politics was in itself highly unusual—most people considered knowledge superior to action, and therefore action could not be used to justify knowledge. Coluccio tried to forestall criticism by invoking our own William of Ockham. Ockham held that the will, not the intellect, is man's highest and most distinctive faculty, that if and when we get to heaven, we shall not sit moonishly contemplating God but actively love Him, and that action matters more than mere knowing. But Dominici refused to accept this for, being a Dominican, he was also a Thomist and an Aristotelian.

Dominici's replies to Coluccio I will only glance at. First came the old chestnut that pagan books turn you into a pagan: each man becomes the thing he reads. Then he goes on to deny that the truths in literature do come from God, because, as Aristotle says, the kind of truth that exists in the mind of God is different: unchanging and universal. This is not as foolish as it sounds, and is still an issue today when we argue for example that Hamlet's problems have a universal validity. Secondly, says Dominici, reading secular books amounts to 'gaping at vanities and is a kind of infidelity to God'. Thirdly, pagan literature introduces errors and heresy. For example, Plato teaches that wives should be held in common, while the myth of Perseus slaying the Gorgon has reappeared as St. George and the dragon, thus reducing the life of a remarkable Christian soldier to the level of cheap fable. It would be pleasant to report that the Florentines, a fair-minded people, recognized that Coluccio's arguments were stronger and made Dominici hang his head in shame. What actually happened was that Dominici was given a Cardinal's hat, and Italy was swept by a wave of anti-humanism. Up in Mantua a prominent layman toppled a statue of Virgil into the river Mincio, as though symbolically to destroy every pagan book. There the matter might have ended for a generation or two had not war broken out in 1390 and put the whole problem in a new light.

The aggressor was Giangaleazzo Visconti, Duke of Milan. His banner showed a coiled viper swallowing a man whole, and he himself wanted to swallow Italy whole. He started by poisoning his uncle, as Chaucer for one believed, then grabbed northern Italy and sent his steel-cased cavalry pouring over the Apennines against Bologna and Florence. He worked out a fabulous family tree which traced him back to Aeneas and (though he was a very plain man) to Venus too for good measure. He launched a propaganda drive to the effect that he, the Duke, was restoring the Empire, and thereby unity. Any city which tried to stop him was being selfish and bloody-minded.

At first Florence, though weaker in arms and men, did not do too badly thanks to her English general, Sir John Hawkwood, but Hawkwood died in 1394. Then Florence found herself ringed and alone. It had become a war of ideologies. Whereas the Empire was a magic word that stirred men's hearts, Florence's battle-cry of civic liberty had little or no magic. Giangaleazzo spoke for many when he described a republic as really the tyranny of the mob. Coluccio realized this. He saw that if he was to counter Milanese propaganda and boost Florentine morale he must be able to define freedom, give examples of freedom producing good results, and the only source for this was the past. It was do or die now, and the quasi-ban on pagan books would have to be disregarded.

Coluccio and his friends plunged into Roman history. They read Livy and Sallust and above all Cicero. They found that the Roman Republic had achieved prodigious things, and under a form of government much like their own. From this period they collected texts and definitions, speeches and examples which Coluccio wove into propaganda so effective that Giangaleazzo said it did him more harm than a thousand horsemen. The great classical age, said Coluccio, had been the Republic, not the Empire. He and his friends even went back to the founding of Florence and discovered a text which showed—falsely as it happens—that the town had been founded by veterans of Sulla, therefore under the Republic, before the Caesars had swept away freedom. Here was a direct link. Instead of being alone in a world of imperialists, Florentines had found an ally—one in the past but an ally no less. They began calling themselves 'new Romans', a tag which even Giangaleazzo accepted, using it, however, in derision.

Meanwhile, the war went worse than ever. In 1400 Florence was blockaded. Famine came, and plague, and near-bankruptcy, and the Fraticelli, who swarmed over Italy, shaggy men in white Ku-Klux-Klan hoods, crying 'Repent for the end of the world is nigh'. They preached peace at any price, even Gianga-leazzo's price of enslavement. Against all this Florence held out for fourteen weary months. But she could not hold out indefinitely.

Then, quite suddenly in September 1402, the Duke of Milan caught a fever and died. His army split up, his empire fell to pieces, and Florence was saved. It seemed that the town had won a great victory, and in a way she had, not on the battle-field, but through the morale of her citizens, and the mystic tie with the past. If they had survived, it was as new Romans. The question of whether or not to read the classics was now resolved. These books clearly held the recipe of success, and could not be ignored. In 1405 when the Florentines captured pro-Milanese Pisa, among their loot was a copy of the *Pandects*, the most complete collection of Roman law, and this precious manuscript was carried in triumph through the streets of Florence, cheered like a hero.

There were very few classical manuscripts in private hands in Florence, so the next step was to track them down in the monastery libraries of Europe. A Florentine named Niccolò Niccoli took charge of this. He was a friend of Coluccio but quite different in character: very handsome, very fussy about the whiteness of his table linen and the cut of his long scarlet dress, and so sensitive his nerves went on edge, we are told, at 'the braying of an ass, the grating of a saw, and the squeaking of a trapped mouse'. Niccolò led a retired life on a small private income. What interested him most in classical literature was its beautiful style, which made churchmen's Latin seem coarse and clumsy. He did not write books himself, being unable to satisfy his own high standards. Nor did he marry, perhaps for the same reason. Instead, he kept a mistress named Benvenuta. Niccolò's serious-minded younger friend Leonardo Bruni was shocked at this. He called the girl Malvenuta and trotted out some splendid Latin boo-phrases: 'flagitium tantum, tam atrox, tam detestabile'. Bruni was alarmed that the old charge 'Pagan books lead to pagan morals' would be levelled at Florence's scholarly laymen.

Niccolò, being as I have said a retiring sort of man, needed someone enterprising actually to hunt down manuscripts. He found him in Poggio Bracciolini, a gay, energetic young notary with no respect for anyone—the kind of man who offers to go anywhere and do anything. Though no great lover of the clergy, Poggio earned a living as papal secretary and in 1414 crossed the Alps with Pope John XXIII to the Council of Constance, where—you remember Gibbon's phrase—'the most scandalous charges were suppressed; the vicar of Christ was only accused of piracy, murder, rape, sodomy, and incest'. John was found guilty, deposed, imprisoned, and Poggio found himself without a job. It was then that he began one of the oddest treasure hunts imaginable—not for gold or silver or spices, but for dusty old parchment, stacked away among the cobwebs and dust. He visited Langres in France and Einsiedeln in Switzerland and Reichenau in Austria. In the abbey of St. Gall he made his first major find: the full text of Quintilian's *Art of Oratory*, which gave a complete picture of the Roman educational system. Poggio wrote to Florence:

I truly believe that, had we not come to the rescue, this man Quintilian must speedily have perished; for it cannot be imagined that a man magnificent, polished, elegant, urbane and witty could much longer have endured the squalor of the prison-house in which I found him, the savagery of his gaolers, the forlorn filth of the place. He was indeed a sad sight: ragged, like a condemned criminal, with rough beard and matted hair, protesting by his expression and dress against the injustice of his sentence. He seemed to be stretching out his hands, calling upon the Romans, demanding to be saved from so undeserved a fate. It was hard indeed that he who had preserved the lives of many by his eloquence and aid should now find no redresser of his wrongs, no saviour from the unjust punishment awaiting him.

Poggio copied the manuscript in thirty-two days and sent it to Florence. Other finds followed. A Latin cookery book turned up next to Lucretius' sublime poem, *De rerum natura*. Pliny's *Natural History* was spotted up in Lübeck, and Niccolò bought it through an agent in the Medici bank. At the same time Florentines were arranging for Greek manuscripts to be shipped from Constantinople: Plautus and Cicero's letters were joined by Homer and Plato and Thucydides, not to mention the geographers and cosmologists and medical writers. In less than a generation Florence came into a literary heritage of unprecedented richness. We have to imagine a hundred Dead Sea scrolls discovered all at once, or a meteorite striking the earth, and inside the Loeb series. That was the effect, though of course there was nothing neat and tidy about it. For example, Poggio lent his Lucretius to Niccolò, who was notorious for not returning books—he was a generous lender too and once had 200 books out on loan. Finally, Poggio had to write Niccolò a somewhat plaintive note, saying in effect: 'It's now 12 years since I lent you my Lucretius. I'd rather like to read it. After all I *did* discover it.'

The Florentines were exultant about these finds, but they were also overwhelmed. In philosophy alone they were faced with a dozen different schools: Pythagoreans, Epicureans, Cynics, Neo-Platonists, Stoics, and many others. Even in one field they could not assimilate everything. So inevitably they selected, and this they did according to their needs. We shall come in a moment to what they did select, but first I want to notice one thing they ignored: what we today consider the brightest jewel, namely, Greek tragedy. To start with, it was written in difficult Greek, and without a dictionary the Florentines found those clipped, one-line dialogues, those choruses crammed with images as puzzling as we did at school. Then again, the subject-matter proved difficult. Oedipus tearing out his eyes and wandering helpless from Thebes to Colonus —the whole notion of the gods toying with men—none of this fitted in with their Christian view of life. Most important of all, the Florentines did not feel a need to see events in tragic terms. They had won a victory, their bankers and merchants were doing well and they were filled with confidence. The blind Oedipus held no interest. Nor for that matter did the cynical history of Tacitus, whom they also ignored.

What then did interest them? The answer is, the Greeks and Romans in recognizable situations, as living persons striving and achieving. And the first thing that struck the Florentines was the immense importance they had attached to will. Achilles and Odysseus, Alcibiades and the heroes sung by Pindar—each felt he must always excel and surpass himself, that a man wins his manhood through unflagging effort and unflinching risk. So too with the Romans, though more soberly —Camillus and Scipio Africanus, Pompey, and a legion of others had forged their own destinies through driving will. This impressed the Florentines all the more because they had been brought up on books like Boethius's *Consolations of Philosophy*: the world bristling with hostile forces, no good man able to cope, the only solution resignation, surrender of the will. Will in Christian authors usually meant God's will, and virtue consisted in complying with that. Since God's will was distressingly inscrutable, the result too often had been passivity, drift, and a static society.

The Florentines adopted the Roman name for this driving will, the power in a man that makes him what he is. They called it *virtus*. It differed from any Christian virtue, even from fortitude, for whereas fortitude is a kind of passive courage in face of pain or adversity, *virtus* is very positive. *Virtus* was the single most important element in the classical ideal evolved in Florence.

The next characteristic which impressed the Florentines was the ancients' strong civic sense—their public-spiritedness—to be seen in Socrates fighting barefoot through the winter campaign at Potidaea, Cicero hurrying back from retirement to try and save the Republic, Pericles adorning Athens with public buildings. This strengthened and extended in range the Florentines' own tradition of service. It helped to end political vendettas, it led to patronage of artists, and to the sort of remark made by Alberti, when he claimed that the outside of a house was the most important, because it was the part all citizens could enjoy.

I am not suggesting that patriotism was a new thing, only the modes of patriotism, even the language, as I will try to show now. Leonardo Bruni—the same who called Benvenuta Malvenuta—had, as a young man, lived through the traumatic war with Milan. He experienced feelings of patriotism but was unable to express them until he came across a Greek booklet in praise of Athens. It was a third-rate work by a rhetor named Aristides, but it answered Bruni's needs. He dashed off a Latin equivalent, applying to Florence the praises Aristides bestowed on Athens: healthy climate, clean streets, hard-working citizens, etc. Certain adjustments were necessary. Aristides had praised Athens' position on the sea; Bruni considered inland was better. Look, he said not without a certain treachery, look at a city like Athens—hopelessly exposed position on the sea, hence its downfall. Bruni's *Laudatio* is the most beautiful book in praise of Florence ever written, the first to be inspired by a Greek model, and an example of how a Greek's civic sense was imparted to the Florentines.

The third element enthroned in the classical ideal was versatility. Whereas the Middle Ages had been a period of specialists based on the guild system, the ancients had tended to be all-rounders. We think of Pericles, of Julius Caesar both general and historian, of Pliny who wrote on everything from painting to volcanoes. There had been no distinction then between clerics thinking theoretical truths and laymen engaged in lower, practical concerns. Both were inter-related, for example, in Cicero. To critics who doubted his ability for philosophic work after a life-long political career Cicero replied: 'I have been studying philosophy most earnestly at the very time when I seemed to be doing so least.' This reply became famous in Florence, with its implication that a man's thoughts and theories should grow out of practical experience. Such an approach was specially important in the arts. It did not escape notice that Socrates had earned his living as a sculptor—evidently a good one, for his statue of the Three Graces was preserved in the Acropolis. Without the ideal of a versatile artist who thinks, we might not have had the work of Leonardo da Vinci or Michelangelo.

Mainly from these three elements the Florentines fashioned

their ideal of classical man: strong-willed, public-spirited, versatile. And in order to transmit it, they took a bold step. They altered that most conservative of systems, the educational and gave a prominent place to classical literature in the widest sense, including moral philosophy. They called the new course *litterae humaniores*, learning more humane than previous disciplines in that it dealt direct with human beings.

This decision to study literature was taken in 1428 and must surely rank as one of the turning-points in Western civilization. But it has to be said at once that the classics were not studied as pure literature. Coluccio defined the humanities as 'moral learning'. Style interested him too, for without a convincing style a man couldn't give effect to his driving will. But the main interest was undoubtedly moral situations. Classical literature provided a vast repertory of these: men faced by dilemmas—the infidelity of a wife, the dishonour of a daughter, revolution, the loss of a patron's favour, such as Nero's for Seneca, and so on. These had an immediate appeal for laymen, lacking in Christian hagiography, with its emphasis on the next life and its easy solutions in the form of miracles.

Interest in morals inevitably led to comparisons. Leonardo Bruni retold an incident he had found in the Greek historian Appian. It concerns King Seleucus of Syria, whose son Antiochus falls violently in love with his father's beautiful young second wife. Antiochus controls his passion, but falls sick and longs to die. Seleucus calls the doctor, who seems to have been a psychiatrist. 'Your son's disease is love,' he tells Seleucus, 'but a love that is hopeless.' The doctor only dares to hint at the lady in question, but Seleucus understands. Instead of storming into a rage and pulling out daggers, he gives his wife to Antiochus, who promptly recovers and all three live happily after. Bruni then compares Seleucus with a well-known figure in Italian history, Tancred of Naples. Tancred had a beautiful daughter named Ghismonda, of whom he was jealously possessive. When a Neapolitan noble started courting the girl, Tancred had the suitor strangled, whereupon Ghismonda died of grief. Bruni concluded that 'in humanity and kindness of heart the ancient Greeks were far in advance of Christians'. Notice the wording: 'in humanity and kindness of heart'. Bruni never doubted that Christian revelation imparted truths far higher than any known to the pagans, but did Christians live up to them, and the great precept of charity?

The study of literature made then for tolerance and exalted

the solidarity of all human beings, whatever their religious code. At its best this became a generous desire to discover truths which Christianity held in common with other religions. We have one example of this in a pair of pictures by Filippino Lippi, now in the National Gallery. The first shows a familiar enough subject—Moses striking water from the rock—but the second is unusual. A bull seems to be prancing in mid-air, while down below worshippers beat drums, blow horns, clash cymbals, and generally go through the motions of religious enthusiasm. The worshippers are by the way derived from a Bacchic relief, one of countless such borrowings from the antique, and the painting seems to me a very lovely one. Now we know from an episode in Pliny that the bull is meant to be the Egyptian god Apis, who annually rose from the Nile at Memphis in this form and disported himself in the air. But the worship of Apis is not condemned as superstition or mass delusion, it is recognized as a sincere approach to a God who had not yet chosen to manifest himself as man. Moses is the link between the pictures, for he was a scholar of the Egyptian hierophants. Both miracles are seen as foreshadowing the ultimate miracle of the Resurrection. Whatever we think of this as a piece of comparative religion, we cannot but admire it as an expression of tolerance.

Another field where the classical ideal left its mark was wit and humour. Cicero's *De Oratore* made an analysis of these subjects and cited many witty anecdotes. Plutarch, Aulus Gellius, and Macrobius all left collections of funny stories. The Middle Ages had known buffoonery but not wit and humour in this sense. These made their reappearance with the Florentines, directly inspired by classical models. Lorenzo de' Medici and his friend Matteo Franco are riding through Tuscany and stop at an inn. They ask for a drink and the landlord pours them what he calls a fine old wine. They swallow a mouthful, and find it palpably new. 'Hmm, very old. It seems to have attained second childhood.' A different tone, but in the same tradition of terse wit, is seen in Cosimo de' Medici's profound remark: 'Every artist paints himself.' Poggio's wit is more licentious. He visits Baden, with its spa and curative baths. He is intrigued (and as an Italian surprised) to find both sexes taking the baths together and even engaging in aquatic dinner parties, dainties being served on floating tables. 'What are these baths meant to cure?' Poggio asks himself drily. 'Doubtless a low birth rate.' Poggio collected funny stories all his life. One he picked up on his visit to England. It is not very funny, but it is perhaps the first story gleaned by a visitor to these shores and therefore worth repeating. An Irish sea-captain is caught in a storm. As the waves rise higher, so he makes vows to the Blessed Virgin if she will save him and the crew—he will give up swearing, make a novena, and so on. But still the waves crash over the heaving ship. At last he throws himself on his knees. 'Blessed Mary, I'll give you a candle as high as the mast.' One of the sailors points out that a candle like that could not be made with all the wax in Ireland. 'Hold your tongue,' says the captain, 'who's to know that?'

If we were to ask which classical author most influenced the Florentines, the answer, in the fields of philosophy and science, would certainly be Plato. But if we are thinking of the Florentine character and way of life, and of civilization generally, the answer must be the historians. Their influence and the rise of the historical method in Florence are so important that I want to dwell on them at some length.

In fourteenth-century Florence records of the past were scanty, edifying, and often fanciful. One chronicle tells us that the wife of Catiline attended mass in a certain Florentine church. By my reckoning that would have been about ninety years before the Last Supper. These chronicles were wrapped in gloom. One Florentine defined history as an account of the misfortunes and disasters that overtake mankind—which sounds like the Late Night Final. When the Arno flooded in November 1333, drowning 300 Florentines, Giovanni Villani describes the havoc but instead of inquiring the cause makes this comment: 'God pronounced judgment on us for our outrageous sins.'

In this kind of chronicle man is seen as a pawn, at the mercy of events. Greek and Roman historians, on the other hand, took quite a different approach, based on their more positive attitude to the will. Leonardo Bruni studied them closely and took Livy and Thucydides as his special models when he began to write the history of Florence about 1412. He therefore abandons chronicling by years, which made the year more important than human beings, and he sees the wars and vendettas of the past not as God-given punishments but as man-made strivings. They form a pattern. They are part of man's struggle to achieve political freedom. Bruni sees history as a single process whereby the Florentines have evolved those precious civic liberties enshrined in the Republic.

Bruni's *History* written in classical Latin, has some dull pages and too many Thucydidean speeches, but it is an extraordinarily important work, for it marks the change from history as something static, unconnected as a heap of annual registers, into a purposive movement. Bruni was the first Christian to study the past in order to discover how he and his fellow citizens had come to be as they were. When the history was finished, the Florentines placed a copy of the weighty tome in the Palazzo Vecchio as a kind of spiritual foundation-stone and—an unusual honour, for they were tight with money—they dispensed Bruni and his sons from paying income-tax during their lifetime.

You will remember that Hesiod and Ovid propound a theory of history whereby an age of gold is followed by an age of silver, then of bronze, finally of iron. Dante knew the theory through Virgil's fourth eclogue, where it takes a cyclical form—the world may hope to return from its present age of iron to a golden age, in all essentials like the first. The fifteenth-century Florentines adopted this theory with great eagerness, because it seemed to bring them closer to those classical figures they had come to admire—distant and intriguing as Rousseau's noble savages, but these were noble sages. So we find the Platonic Academy being formed and dining on Plato's birthday, 7 November, not just to commemorate the event, but as it were to bring Plato back to life in the person of Ficino, who was addressed as 'another Plato' or 'Plato redivivus'. Lorenzo because of his love of woods and streams was identified with Pan, Botticelli with the Greek painter Apelles because of his genius as a draughtsman—and this identification led Botticelli to the choice of at least two subjects: the *Calumny* and the *Birth of Venus*.

At first sight all this is very strange. It was not a mere dressing up, not pageantry, but something much more potent. Poetic imagination was at work and, as we know from Proust, this faculty cannot work on the present moment, nor yet upon the past *tout pur*, but only on the past when it is entangled in the reality of the present. A unique kind of joy is then experienced, a release from time, and a foretaste of immortality. The little madeleine in Florence might be a newly unearthed coin or cameo, a statue, even an astronomical clock which Lorenzo commissioned to the exact specifications of one built by Archimedes. It might be a real building in classical style, or even an imaginary classical-style town, such as Filarete drew up in 1464. Filarete describes a visitor walking through this town, full of admiration and saying, 'My lord, I seem to see again the noble buildings that were once in Rome and those that we read were in Egypt. It seems to me that on seeing those noble buildings I have been reborn—*mipare rinascere*.' One of the first uses of the Renaissance metaphor.

If the cyclical theory sometimes led to ecstasy, more often it acted as a stimulus to hard work. It helps to explain the extraordinary fruitfulness of the classical ideal. In one of his letters Ficino compares his own revival of Platonic philosophy to the rebirth of grammar, poetry, rhetoric, painting, sculpture, architecture, music, and astronomy which had been accomplished in his century. Ficino omits history, and the reason I think is that history was so fundamental to the process in every field that it escaped notice.

Twice before the fifteenth century there had been golden ages, and in both idealization played a key role. It is worth glancing briefly at them, to see what light they throw on the Florentine phenomenon. The first age was fifth-century Athens, and the ideal here was the heroic ideal embodied in the *Iliad* and the *Odyssey*, written down under Pisistratus and adopted as the basis of Athenian education. The heroic ideal exalted adventure and the reckless struggle against odds, it gave a prominent place to friendship between men, and it confirmed the Athenians in their taste for war. The heroic ideal could be said perfectly to complement the more prudent and refined sides of the Athenian character, as embodied in the doctrine of the mean and the value accorded to art.

The other golden age is the late Republic and principate. We sometimes forget just how much the Romans of that period admired Greece. They used Greek for serious conversation, for philosophy, for love-making. Julius Caesar's last words were not 'Et tu, Brute', but 'καὶ σύ τέκνον;—Not you, my child?' But the Romans idealized the Greeks for quite the opposite reason that the Athenians idealized Homer's heroes. The Romans knew themselves to be masters on the battlefield, in administration, and practical concerns like building roads and baths and arenas—what *they* lacked was finesse and philosophy and art, which is why Cicero went to school with Plato and Terence with Menander. Both the Athenians and Romans, then, were subconsciously seeking the qualities they lacked and which would bring them to fulfilment. The same held true of Florence. I say 'subconsciously' because there seems to be no sign that they weighed the pros and cons of the various elements they selected. It was almost an instinctive process, and this seems to lend support to theories of human progress.

Despite these resemblances, the golden age in Florence differed from its predecessors in two important ways. First, by the very long interval—more than 1,400 years—separating the composite model from its imitators. This increased the impression of something truly prodigious, and also imparted a sense of guilt that there had been such a long neglect. Both enormously strengthened the impulse to achievement. Secondly, Florence itself had a more powerful contribution to make than either Athens or Rome—namely, Christianity. At every point Christianity informed, purified, modified, and sometimes retarded the classical ideal; but this is too complex a subject to pursue tonight.

As I have said, the classical ideal enthroned by the Florentines was extremely selective, and it is interesting to ask whether the ideal would have been markedly different had it emerged elsewhere. Alexander the Great here provides a clue. Like the Athenians Alexander's favourite book was the *Iliad*, but whereas for the Athenians a Homeric hero was a man who recognized that he was only a man and could never be a god, Alexander, we know, took an opposite view. We find similar happenings in fifteenth-century Italy. Sigismondo Malatesta, despot of Rimini, built a church with a sound classical façade, but inside ambition ran wild. In 200 places he displayed his initial, interlaced with that of his mistress; the Malatesta elephant trumpeted his fame, virtues sang his praises, and he was even depicted on the ceiling rising into heaven to take his place as one of the stars. In Rome also, Roderigo Borgia took the name of Pope Alexander, after Alexander the Great; Giuliano della Rovere that of Julius Caesar; and Leo X on a famous occasion refused to go into mourning: 'I am not', he explained, 'like other men, but rather a demi-god—*non ut homo sed ut semideus.*' Without Florence we should have caught quite a different echo from the classical past: the thump of legions, the massed people with outstretched arms shouting, 'Hail Caesar!'

And what of Florence? Which way would she have gone without the classical ideal? I doubt whether the republic would have possessed the self-confidence and unity to survive amid despotic enemies, and I doubt whether we should have had the quality of idealism in Florentine work—idealism after all implies an ideal. We have to remember just how shrewd, hardheaded, and matter of fact Florentines were—had to be, as bankers and merchants. I believe development would have taken place along the line of Sacchetti's *novelle*, with a strong tone of irony and perhaps also a touch of the cynicism to be seen later, when the golden age is past, in Machiavelli's *Mandragola*. It was of course precisely the Florentine's hard-headed qualities —his skill at double-entry book-keeping and building and dyeing cloth—which prevented idealism becoming wan or moonish.

The classical ideal as evolved by Florence became around 1500 our ideal too. We recall Linacre studying Greek with Lorenzo's sons, then teaching it to Thomas More. We recall Colet's journey to Italy, where he learned the historical method, and those first lectures on St. Paul's Epistles, not as pretexts for allegory and dialectics, but as straightforward documents to be understood in terms of the values and language of the first century A.D. We find artists flocking over, among them Torrigiani who broke Michelangelo's nose in a boyish fight, and who made Henry VII's tomb in Westminster Abbey. We in our turn came into the immensely rich heritage, but now it was triple: Greece, Rome, and Florence, with other Italian elements added. If Shakespeare's imagination was fired by Julius Caesar and Coriolanus, and also by Iago and Romeo and the Florentine Cassio, part of the reason is that they all arrived on the same import shipment.

Soon we in Britain were interpreting the classics for ourselves. The ideal we formed was not markedly different from the Florentines', though we came to attach more importance to the athlete, to cold baths, and to lyric poetry. I think we can claim that the classical ideal has been pretty faithfully embodied in our civilization. The elements I have mentioned tonight—a driving will, civic pride, versatility, the study of literature, tolerance, wit, and humour—we accept as almost too obvious for comment. Even the present decline in classical studies I interpret as a triumph, not a defeat of the classical ideal: the message has been learned, the transfusion made. This emerges also in our attitude to other kinds of renewal: the Gothic revival, the pre-Raphaelites, nineteenth-century French romanticism—we see them as essentially fringe movements, deviations from our central tradition.

The brightest light casts the darkest shadow. The shadow here is that the classical past can no longer act as a catalyst. If we accept that a grafting from another garden is necessary in order to produce Botticelli's unique golden apples, from where is the next graft to come? You will all have your own answer. Myself, I should say from the East. In a world grown noisy and nervous there is obviously a special virtue in self-possession and stillness. As axes fall on the oaks of England, as factories and roads drive the soul from nature, a new value also attaches to making our interiors places of beauty. In a crowded world, where the large-scale gesture is obsolescent, a new importance attaches to doing little things with style and feeling, as the Japanese do when serving tea. I also think that we have much to learn from the East about the role of women, a point where the classical ideal is notoriously inadequate. But this is mere speculation and I would like to turn back finally to my central theme, the classical ideal, and leave you with a true story.

One hot summer's day in the middle of the *quattrocento* a man in his fifties was travelling from Santa Fiora to Rome. He was a Tuscan—though not a Florentine—and obviously a great lord, for he was surrounded by courtiers and attentive servants. Because he suffered from gout and rheumatism he was not riding a horse or mule, but was carried on a chair shoulder-high between horsemen. He had some endearing qualities, notably a love of nature. He would stop to admire blue flax fields, the scarlet of wild strawberries, a clump of beech-trees; and he liked picnics, especially if a fresh-caught trout was served. But he was rather a stern irascible man who had formed his political opinions in Germany and was the very opposite of democratic. As the procession wound through the hills they came on a herd of cows and a cowherd. The cowherd was awestruck by the fine men, by the glitter of gold and scarlet. He shuffled uneasily and then, thinking the heat must have made the important-looking lord thirsty, he milked the nearest cow, catching the milk in his own bowl, which he then offered to the lord. As I have said, this man had little time for the peasantry, his health was poor, and the bowl was black with dirt and grease. He was inclined to motion the procession on. But he did not. His stern expression unexpectedly changed to a smile. He was a classical scholar and he was recalling a story in Plutarch about a peasant who had offered water in his two hands to Artaxerxes, King of Persia. So now the lord in the chair took the bowl and put it to his lips, pretending to drink, then handed it round to his courtiers, while the cowherd beamed. The story sums up much of what I have been trying to say tonight: history giving an edge to an otherwise flat experience, the classical ideal helping a man in a small matter to surpass himself. Indeed, you may think the story specially apt, for the man in the chair was Pope.

# MARIA EDGEWORTH:
# A BICENTENARY LECTURE

*By* LORD EVANS, M.A., L.L.D., D.LIT., F.R.S.L.

*(Read 23 February 1967)*

*Baroness Stocks, B.Sc., LL.D., Litt.D., F.R.S.L., in the Chair*

IT is many years now since I inflicted a discourse on this distinguished company. When the invitation came I could not resist the honour of doing so again, especially under the Chairmanship of my valued friend, Lady Stocks. Yet I fear that all this enthusiasm has placed me in an invidiously false position. All I really knew about Maria Edgeworth was that she had a very special relation with her father, that she had written *Castle Rackrent* and some children's books, that Scott admired her, and that she and her father had written about education. I realize that there may be in this audience genuine authorities, and even descendants of the great and multifarious Edgeworth family, and so I approach the whole evening with trepidation.

In all honesty, I must confess that it is some years since she or her work impinged on my mind in any way, and now it is the bicentenary of her birth. Of course, some members of this audience, learned though it is, may be similarly placed. It would be interesting on an occasion of this kind to have some sort of literary lie detector, which would register how much even this reading audience had been indulging in Maria Edgeworth or in any other writer whose centenary emerges.

I decided I would begin my researches in the library of the *Athenaeum*. After all, that was where Macaulay wrote his *History of England*. The Athenaeum had indeed a shelf full of Maria Edgeworth, but they were placed up very high in a case in the lounge and, as it were, to secure inaccessibility, the case was protected at the base by a wide settee. No library ladder could reach them, and to judge from appearances they had not been reached for many a year. Then I recalled that Macaulay had at his service a page boy who would fetch books from the London Library. In these days of diminished services, when no page boys are available, I set out for the London Library and with some moderate success. But at last and as ever, I had to fall back on the British Museum Reading Room.

Maria Edgeworth was born on 1 January 1767, and so this year we celebrate, a little late, her bicentenary. The most important thing in her life was that she belonged to a great Irish family and all that is best in her work derives from Ireland. This Irish origin and Irish allegiance mean that she does not fit into the chronology of English literature: there is a certain timelessness about her. There is about the whole family.

Though she was of an Irish family, she spent her girlhood in England. This I think was regrettable, for if this lecture has any theme it is that she was best when left to herself, and that the best in herself came from Ireland. Not all her biographers share this view. In an early biography by Miss Zimmern we read: 'Ireland is not amongst those countries that arouse in the hearts of strangers a desire to pitch their tents, and to judge from the readiness with which her own children leave her, we cannot suppose that they found her a fascinating land.' As a child she paid a visit to Ireland, but from 8 to 15 she was in English girls' seminaries, first at Derby and then in Miss Davis's very superior establishment in Upper Wimpole Street. There is one incident about her schooldays most revealing for those interested in education as a whole. The Derby establishment was a modest one, run by a Mrs. Lataffière, but she had a husband who, for the fun of it, gave this little girl private lessons in French and Italian. As a result, she found that when she came to Miss Davis's she could write out a whole quarter's exercises at once 'keeping them strung together in her desk, and while the other girls were labouring at their tasks, she had all that time for reading what she pleased to herself, and when the French master came round for the exercises, had only to unstring hers and present it'. The moral, leaving aside that taint of priggishness which I fear is never far from Maria, is that in education if there is a willing and alert intelligence and a dedicated teaching mind, everything can be achieved and without these very little.

From her earliest days Maria was fascinated by that extraordinary man, her father, Richard Lovell Edgeworth. I may as well make a clear declaration now, for it will become apparent later, I do not understand him, and ultimately I must confess I do not find him wholly attractive. He contributes to this sense of timelessness of the Edgeworths. He is irrepressible, often incredible, and with all his preaching and didacticism often like some character out of Irish comedy. Yet one must remember

Byron's testimony and Byron was not easily taken in: 'a fine old fellow—intelligent, vehement, vivacious, and full of life'. Of course, Byron does also comment that he 'talked loud and long'. He was, let it be in justice admitted, a very ingenious and clever man. To me he never seems quite real. There is, for instance his matrimonial record. As an undergraduate he married a Miss Elers, not because he liked her very much but, as he said, he found himself 'insensibly entangled and so completely that I could not find any honourable means of extraction'. Despite all his later moralizings he was a wild character during these years. My own theory is that he was utterly unsuited for the classical education that was imposed on him, as he was also unsuited for the later legal studies which were imposed on him. He was naturally suited for a scientific and technological education. Had such been available I think he might have been a very great man. As it was, he had a number of ingenious discoveries. They were not co-ordinated for England had no scientific background to give him support.

The marriage with Miss Elers was not a success. Maria was the second child and there were in all five children. After which, the lady died. Mr. Edgeworth had another candidate very ready for the matrimonial office, Honora Sneyd of Lichfield, whom he married in Lichfield Cathedral four months after his wife's death. Edgeworth had long known the Lichfield circle, including Thomas Day, the egregious author of *Sandford and Merton*, who had a great influence on Edgeworth, particularly in his later pedagogic studies. Edgeworth was a favourite not only with Honora but with Anna Seward, her cousin, who wrote verse and was the 'Swan of Lichfield', and for jealousy or other reasons she was one of the few people to speak of Edgeworth with real bitterness: 'the specious, the false, the cruel, the murderous Edgeworth, who cankered first and then crushed to earth the finest of human flowers'. All this circle is difficult to penetrate, especially Mr. Day. He was himself in love with Honora but willingly assigned her to his friend. Anyway, Day had other occupations: he had taken two girls from a Foundling Hospital, Lucretia and Sabrina, to educate them up and see which was the more worthy to marry him.

The marriage with Honora was a success. She added two children to the family and then died of consumption. Maria was still safely tucked away at the Mrs. Lataffière seminary, learning French and Italian from the husband of Mrs. Lataffière, but her father was not too busy to send instructions:

It would be very agreeable to me, my dear Maria, to have letters from you familiarly. I wish to know what you would like, and what you dislike; I wish to communicate with you what little knowledge I have acquired that you may have a tincture of every species of literature, and form a taste by choice and not by chance.

Happy though the marriage with Honora was, I still find Mr. Edgeworth a puzzling and incongruous character. As he sat by Honora's bedside immediately after her death, he wrote Maria a letter. Augustus Hare, who is Edgeworth's main biographer, describes it in his *Life and Letters* as a 'touching' letter. It begins with these sentences:

My dear Daughter, at six o'clock on Thursday morning your excellent mother expired in my arms. She now lies dead beside me, and I know I am doing what would give her pleasure, if she were capable of feeling anything, by writing to you at this time to fix her excellent image in your mind.

Edgeworth's next step was to marry Elizabeth Sneyd, his dead wife's sister. He makes it clear that of all Honora's sisters Elizabeth attracted him the least, and that she did not think particularly well of him, but as it was Honora's last wish he enters into matrimony for a third time. A certain delay was occasioned in order to avoid those who opposed marriage to a dead wife's sister, but it was all arranged; Elizabeth was a great success, greater even than Honora. Elizabeth had five sons and four daughters and then, like her sister, died of consumption, and Edgeworth found a fourth, and mercifully let it be recorded a last wife. She was a Miss Beaufort, a rector's daughter, who came into the circle as the illustrator of *The Parent's Assistant*, the volume of stories for children which Maria wrote with help from her father. Elizabeth died in November 1797 and in the spring of 1798 Edgeworth was ready with his proposals to Frances Beaufort. She had two sons and four daughters but she succeeded in surviving her husband and Maria, with whom an attachment of considerable depth developed.

It may be urged that I have given too much attention to Mr. Edgeworth but it is difficult to avoid him. Maria never did, and from all the extant evidence never wanted to. She found herself the centre of his enormous family, and apart from the children other relations were invited to take up permanent residence at Edgeworthstown, the family home in Ireland. She helped to run the estate and at moments of crisis her duties were formidable. As far as we know, only once did she consider life outside the family when suddenly in Paris in 1802 a Swedish nobleman, Mr. Edelcrantz, appeared and offered marriage. In her letters, Maria dismisses the matter as of little consequence; she would not wish to leave her family and she could not bear the life of a Swedish court, but Frances Beaufort, her final step-mother if that is how one describes her, spoke of the matter differently: 'Maria was mistaken as to her own feelings. She refused M. Edelcrantz but she felt much more for him than esteem and admiration; she was exceedingly in love with him.' She adds the interesting comment that 'Mr. Edgeworth left her to decide for herself; but she saw too plainly what she would feel at parting from us. She decided rightly for her own future happiness and for that of her family, but she suffered much at the time and long afterwards.'

Maria spoke as if all her written work owed its inspiration to her father and some biographers, such as Desmond Clarke, have accepted this statement. He writes: 'without her father's help and collaboration it is doubtful if she would have written anything of consequence.' My own view is that kindly and interested though Edgeworth was, his influence was a very doubtful advantage. She wrote one really good book *Castle Rackrent* and she wrote that at Edgeworthstown while her father was away in Dublin. It is said, and it may only be a legend, that Newton would never have mastered his theory of Gravitation had not a plague driven him out of Cambridge. Maria, I submit, would never have written *Castle Rackrent* had not her ebullient father been away from home. Mrs. Barbauld gave a positive assurance that *Castle Rackrent* was written 'without his advice or supervision'. Yet when Maria informed her aunt Mrs. Ruxton on the publication of *Castle Rackrent* she wrote: 'We have begged Johnson (that is the publisher) to send you *Castle Rackrent*. I hope it has reached you? Do not mention to anyone that it is ours.' She awards her father a share in the authorship though he had not written a line.

What would have happened to the Brontës if they had had Edgeworth as a father? Erratic and eccentric though Patrick was he brought them their toy soldiers and let them wander through their fantasy countries alone. Maria was never left alone. The harsh may accuse Patrick Brontë of the cruelty of neglect. Edgeworth exercised another quality: it would be unfair to call it cruelty, because it was unconscious: it was possessiveness, complete and absolute and under that tyranny, however gentle, the artist cannot flourish.

Apart from all her family duties she shared Edgeworth's

interests in educational reform, and it was here that their joint authorship had its most solid basis. Indeed, it was through *The Parent's Assistant* and *Practical Education* that she and her father became famous. *Practical Education* was a joint family venture and it is a remarkable book. It may seem extraordinary that one who was so impulsive and eccentric as Mr. Edgeworth should have thought out so fully so many of these problems in such an original way. In many matters he is far in advance of his time. The egregious Mr. Thomas Day could not have been much help. Edgeworth knew Rousseau and Rousseau's influence is obvious, and he had a close relationship with that 'ingenious man Erasmus Darwin'. Most of the writing of *Practical Education* is by Maria but one must assume that the thinking and direction came from her father. Much is splendid in the volume—kindliness instead of cruelty, individual attention, practical experiment, the sciences, and Chemistry, a chapter specially written by Edgeworth's son. Religion was omitted. It was implied that education was for children of all religious creeds and that these matters could be left to parents. There is little religious emphasis in Maria's work: she is governed rather by her father's rational utilitarian morality. Later she was to suffer from the criticism that her father was irreligious. It is difficult to realize that *Practical Education* was published as early as 1796, and there is much for Maria's claim that no one since Bacon had so treated education as a practical science. The conclusions were based on a formidable amount of reading and study in which Maria fully shared: this is fully demonstrated by the references in the footnotes. If some parts of *Practical Education,* particularly the scientific emphasis, could have been absorbed into the English system, the whole history of England in the nineteenth century might have been different. The following, for instance, is a typical passage:

In Dr. Priestley's History of Vision many experiments may be found which are not above the comprehension of children of ten or eleven years old; we do not imagine that any science can be taught by desultory experiments but we think that a taste for science may early be given by making it entertaining and by exciting young people to exercise their reasoning and inventive faculties upon every object that surrounds.

There are remarkable passages in 'Rewards and Punishments' some of which derive from Rousseau, but there is also much original thinking. For instance, we read, 'The contemplation of a distant punishment, however severe, does not affect the imagination with much terror because there is still a secret hope of escape. Hence it is found from experience that the most sanguinary penal laws have always been ineffectual to restraint from crime.' With Edgeworth's enthusiasm for marriage and large families it is not surprising that he considered the education of a woman in terms of a wife and a mother. One wonders what Maria thought of his views. Private teachers in families are important and should be well paid. 'Opulent families', we read, 'should be prepared to pay £300 a year.' This is a wonderful innovation, especially as it is to be practised before the nineteenth century has begun. Yet despite all this, marriage is the thing. 'From the study of learned languages' we read, 'women by custom fortunately for them, are exempted. Of ancient literature they may in translation, which we acknowledge to be excellent, obtain sufficient knowledge.' Yet *Practical Education* is a solid work, which had some influence in England and on the Continent, and as has already been suggested it would have been fortunate if as far as many of its sections are concerned that influence could have been more extensive. Of the moral stories for children that Maria wrote to go with *Practical Education* I think the kindest thing is to pass them over in silence.

Yet one cannot pass them over in silence for *The Parent's Assistant* and *Moral Tales* and other collections of stories helped greatly to make her reputation. I confess that they are frequently of a solemnity as if they had been written for parents rather than for children.

They must have played some part, and possibly an important part, in the history of education. They were an attempt to change the whole conception of the stories that should be presented to children. They were moral and didactic. They sometimes seem to me as the child's literature of some arid and utilitarian world. It is as if Bentham himself had taken to writing stories for children. So, for instance, in *The Good French Governess* some of us are disappointed as the children themselves when they are taken into the rational toyshop, and yet the individual objects in the rational toyshop have much to commend them and follow the lines that were developed by Maria and her father in *Practical Education* and later by many of those who have experimented with children's toys. The emphasis on the rational element does come more powerfully and grimly into position when the whole mythology of the stories that have entertained children from *Jack the Giant Killer* to the rhymes such as *Three Blind Mice* is abolished as dangerous. One must remember that stories then in circulation and, indeed even to this day, are far more formidable and violent than Mr. Miller's very gentle interpretation of *Alice in Wonderland*.

All the stories show how virtue and industry triumph and how evil and idleness are thoroughly punished. In *Lazy Lawrence* we have the wicked Lawrence who did not work but associated with wicked stable boys and Jem the son of a widow who was honest and worked hard and saves his pony Lightfoot from being sold.

At the end, everyone pleaded for Lawrence, but sound Edgeworthian principles prevailed and were expressed by the farmer: 'Don't ask the lady to speak for him: it's better he should go to Bridewell now, than to the gallows by and by.' So Lawrence went to Bridewell for a month and the 'stable-boy was sent for trial, convicted and transported to Botany Bay for a theft', and we are told that 'as for the hardened wretch, everyone was impatient to have him sent to gaol'.

*The False Key* has the same type of setting. Franklin, the honest pauper, is contrasted in the usual way with Felix the dishonest nephew of the cook. They are both house-boys in the same great house. Felix was the leader in a theft with Corkscrew the butler and to gaol they went, and as Mrs. Pomfret the housekeeper said: 'it was my luck to see them all go by to gaol.' These are not gentle stories: morality is unrelenting. To industry there is no alternative. 'Nothing truly great', we are told, 'can be accomplished without trial and time.'

What one must admit is that Maria's stories did have an influence at the time and records show that they were being continuously reprinted into the present century, though as literature I cannot see that the virtues of *Simple Susan* or of *Rosamund* are easily definable.

*The Moral Tales* were written as an adjunct to the serious educational treatises that Maria and her father had written. The London Library copy has an interesting note that their copy was presented to the Library by Maria Edgeworth's great-niece in November 1915. In the preface we are told:

It has somewhere been said by Johnson that merely to invent a new short story is no small effort to the human understanding. How much more difficult is it to construct stories suited to the early years of youth and, at the same time, conformable to the complicated relations of modern society—fictions that display examples of virtue without initiating the young readers into the ways of vice.

It is interesting to remember that these quiet and moral tales were written during periods of war and rebellion when the

French were landing in Ireland and all the cruelty of the times was visible around the Edgeworth family. When Edgeworth was bringing back his fourth wife, the lady who prepared the illustrations for *The Parents' Assistant*, they passed the suspended corpse of a man hanging between the shafts of a cart. The nineteenth century achieved something in an increase in human relations and who knows that the virtuous 'Simple Susan' and 'Rosamund' and all the others, devious though they may seem, did not have some share in that effect?

This extraordinary family seemed to retain its own life and identity however fierce and boisterous history may be and part of the contribution may have been that through these writings some of their qualities were impressed by their writings on society as a whole.

I find it very difficult to picture Maria, to know what actually went on in her mind. Something one feels must have been suppressed; her relationship with Edelcrantz shows this. As I have said, from all she says, she adored her father and the affection was returned, but he possessed her and it was this possession, genial and kindly though it was, that prevented that release of spirit which might have converted her into a great creative writer. When she had her one proposal of marriage from Edelcrantz her father told her to do as she liked. Is it cynical to suggest that he did so confidently, knowing she could not leave him? Her life was certainly not like that of other women. From 1770 when Maria was 3 until 1812 when she was 45 a child was born into the household every two or three years, usually every two years, and as I have suggested there were other members of the family in permanent residence. When Edgeworth married his fourth wife Frances Beaufort the difference in age between the young bride and Maria was only a few years. Yet it would be very false to deduce from anything I have said that Edgeworth was a domestic tyrant. Apart from his first marriage a great deal of happiness radiated in his circle, and Maria was able to speak frankly of her disapproval of his fourth marriage, though in time she and Frances became close friends.

One of the freest episodes in her life was her visit to Scott. Her father was not with her. Lockhart, in his life of Scott, gives a picture of her: 'full of fun and spirit, a little slight figure, very active, very good humoured and full of enthusiasms'. It is true that in a private communication, a letter to John Wilson who wrote under the name of Christopher North, he was a little more explicit. 'Miss Edgeworth is at Abbotsford and has been for some time; a little, dark, bearded, sharp, withered, active, laughing, talking, impudent, feckless, outspoken, honest, kindly, ultra-Irish body. I like her one day and damn her to perdition the next.' She is a very queer character, and that may be as far as one can get.

But one has to remember that she made a very favourable impression on Byron who wrote in his Journal: 'I had been the lion of 1812: Miss Edgeworth and Madame de Staël were the exhibitions of the succeeding year. . . . A nice little unassuming *Jeannie Deans* looking body, as we Scotch say, and if not handsome certainly not ill looking. Her conversation was as quiet as herself.' Maria was not as generous to his Lordship. 'He may have great talents, but I am sure he has neither a great nor good mind; and I feel dislike and disgust for his Lordship.' It is fair to remember that she wrote this before she met him.

The utilitarian and rationalizing atmosphere of her father's theories imposed its impression on her. She missed the subtle in sentiment and in artistic form. Her references to Jane Austen show that she had no appreciation of the quality of her contemporary. That Jane Austen admired Maria may be assumed as she sent her novels to Edgeworthstown. There is a revealing passage in a letter of Maria's for 10 January 1816:

the authoress of *Pride and Prejudice* has been so good as to send to me a new novel just published, *Emma*. We are reading *France in 1814 and 1815* by young Alison and Mr. Tytler: the first volume is good. We are also reading a book which delights us all, though it is on a subject which you will think little likely to be interesting to us, and on which we have little or no previous knowledge. I bought it on Mr. Brinkley's recommendation and have not repented, Cuvier's *Theory of the Earth*. It is admirably written, with such perfect clearness as to be intelligible to the meanest and satisfactory to the highest intelligence.

*Emma* does not get another mention.

Nor do the other few comments on Jane Austen show any genuine appreciation of her genius. On 21 February 1818, Maria writes to her aunt, Mrs. Ruxton:

I entirely agree with you, my dearest aunt, on one subject, as indeed I generally do on most subjects, but particularly about *Northanger Abbey* and *Persuasion*. The behaviour of the General in *Northanger Abbey*, packing off the young lady without a servant or the common civilities which any bear of a man, not to say gentleman, would have shown, is quite outrageously out of drawing and out of nature. *Persuasion*—excepting the tangled, useless histories of the family in the first fifty pages—appear to me, especially in all that relates to poor Anne and her lover, to be exceedingly interesting and natural. The love and the lover admirably well drawn: don't you see Captain Wentworth, or rather don't you in her place feel him taking the boisterous child off her back as she kneels by the sick boy on the sofa? And is not the first meeting after their long separation admirably well done? And the overheard conversation about the nut? But I must stop: we have got no further than the disaster of Miss Musgrave's jumping off the steps.

I am going on, but very slowly, and not to my satisfaction with my work.

My own belief, as I have already suggested, is that the part of her nature which was imaginative and creative was spontaneous and not intellectual. That she was intellectual need not be denied. Given all else she had to do, the range of her reading is prodigious, but something else had to come alive before the best of herself as an imaginative being could function. When it happened she did not at first recognize its importance.

The outstanding example in her work is *Castle Rackrent*. She discovered intuitively the possibilities in fiction of a local and Irish background. Scott was to do the same for Scotland, and go on doing it with an imagination with which she could not compare. But he was generous in recognizing that she was the innovator as indeed she was. It is when one thinks of how little use Irish writers had made of their own country that the degree of her originality emerges. For the moment, in *Castle Rackrent*, she accepted life and presented it, and the didactic, utilitarian approach of her father was eliminated. In her more formal novels, in *Leonora*, for instance, all the models are English, Addison and Richardson most markedly. But for *Castle Rackrent* it is difficult to discover a model. The writing has the directness and realism of Defoe, and yet it is very different for there is humour and satire as well as observation. Her central character Honest Thady comes, as she herself suggests, from observation.

The only character drawn from the life [she wrote much later in 1834] is Thady himself, the teller of the story. He was an old steward (not very old though, at that time, I added to his age to allow him time for the generations of the family). I heard him when I first came to Ireland, and his dialect struck me, and his character, and I became so acquainted with it that I could think and speak in it without effort; so that when, for mere amusement and without any idea of publishing I began to write the family history as Thady would tell it, he seemed to stand beside me and dictate, and I wrote as far as my pen could go. The characters are all imaginary. Of course, they must have been compounded of persons I had seen, or incidents I had heard, but how compounded I do not know; not by long forethought for I had never thought of them till I began to write, and had made no sort of plan, sketch or framework.

She wrote one other Irish novel, *The Absentee*, much in the mood of *Castle Rackrent*. There are other novels with Irish names and scenes, but with no genuine Irish inspiration. *The Absentee* has more plot than *Castle Rackrent*; it is more consciously built up, but it lacks the highly genuine imaginative qualities of the earlier work. Both novels arise from Maria's reaction to the great Irish landlords, who lived without regard of their tenantry, in a boisterous indulgence, in debt, or in riches from dowries. *Castle Rackrent* has a depth of comic satire which one would not have expected from her more solemn .works. There is, for instance, the description by Thady of Sir Murtagh's wife:

But I always suspected she had Scotch blood in her veins; anything else I could have looked over in her, from regard to the family. She was a strict observer, for self and servants, of Lent, and all fast-days, but not holidays. One of the maids having fainted three times the last day of Lent, to keep soul and body together, we put a morsel of roast beef into her mouth, which came from Sir Murtagh's dinner, who never fasted, not he; but somehow or other it unfortunately reached my lady's ears, and the priest of the parish had a complaint made of it the next day, and the poor girl was forced, as soon as she could walk, to do penance for it, before she could get any peace or absolution, in the house or out of it. However, my lady was very charitable in her own way. She had a charity school for poor children, where they were taught to read and write gratis, and where they were kept well to spinning gratis for my lady in return; for she had always heaps of duty yarn from the tenants, and got all her household linen out of the estate from first to last; for after the spinning the weavers on the estate took it in hand for nothing, because of the looms my lady's interest could get from the Linen Board to distribute gratis. Then there was a bleach-yard near us, and the tenant dare refuse my lady nothing, for fear of a lawsuit Sir Murtagh kept hanging over him about the water-course. With these ways of managing, 'tis surprising how cheap my lady got things done, and how proud she was of it.

When *Castle Rackrent* emerges towards a plot, it becomes improbable, as when Sir Murtagh locks up his wife for years because she will not surrender her diamond cross. But the notes inform us that this is based on a true story. The genius of this book lies in its observation, the first dramatic impact of the young girl, educated in English schools, with her own native Ireland. The notes illuminate the story. Here is a minor example when Thady greets Sir Condy after a domestic crisis: 'Then as I heard my master coming to the passage door, I finished fastening up my slate against the broken pane; and when he came out I wiped down the window-seat with my wig and bade him "good-morrow" as kindly as I could, seeing he was in trouble.'

Let us leave Sir Condy and his domestic crisis and turn to the footnote:

Wigs were formerly used instead of brooms in Ireland for sweeping or dusting tables, stairs, etc. The Editor doubted the fact till he saw a labourer of the old school sweep down a flight of stairs with his wig; he afterwards put it on his head again with the utmost composure, and said 'Oh, please your honour, it's never a bit the worse.'

It must be acknowledged that these men are not in any danger of catching cold by taking off their wigs occasionally, because they usually have fine crops of hair growing under their wigs. The wigs are often yellow, and the hair which appears from beneath them black; the wigs are usually too small, and are raised up by the hair beneath, or by the ears of the wearers.

The strength and spontaneity which come out of these two novels shows what Maria could do when she was left to herself. It can, of course, be argued that without the dynamic father she would have done nothing at all. He urged her to write, but she could not write at her best when he was near, in the same way some of the happiest moments of her life, though she may not have known it, were spent when he was absent, and when she wrote there was usually parental direction at hand.

I have already quoted Lockhart on Maria's visit to Scott. This must have been one of the happiest episodes of her life. She was for once completely free of the solemn precepts and moral attitudes which her father had imposed on her. Certainly, nothing shows Scott in a happier and more generous mood.

Scott was completely devoid of envy, of all the irritable qualities which we associate with writers. There is a memorable charm in his note that lay waiting for her on her Edinburgh visit. The Laird of Staffa and certain of his clansmen were coming to sing Highland boat songs that very evening: 'and if you will come,' writes Scott, 'as the Irish should to the Scotch, without any ceremony, you will hear what is perhaps more curious than mellifluous. The man returns to the Isles tomorrow.' All this only two years before the crisis in Scott's own life. Lockhart, not

MARIA EDGEWORTH: A BICENTENARY LECTURE 53

easily moved, is a witness of the great impression that Maria made on Scott.

August 1923 [he writes] was one of the happiest in Scott's life. Never did I see a brighter day at Abbotsford than that on which Miss Edgeworth arrived there. Never can I forget her look and accent when she received him by the archway and exclaimed: 'Everything about you is exactly what one ought to have had wit enough to dream.'

Day after day, so long as she could remain, her host had always some new plan of . . . gaiety. One day there was fishing on the Cauldshield Loch, and a dinner on the heathery bank. Another, the whole party feasted by Thomas the Rhymer's waterfall in the glen, and the stone on which Maria sat that day was ever afterwards called 'Edgeworth's stone'. Thus a fortnight passed—and the vision closed. Miss Edgeworth never saw Abbotsford again.

She lived on to be 82 and into the Victorian age. She continued to write even after her father's death. His memoirs were published and completed as he had directed, and there were novels popular in their day. *Helen* was published in 1834, forty years since she first ventured forth with *Letters for Literary Ladies* and seventeen years since her last novel. It is alleged that Mrs. Gaskell thought it 'one of the best of all English novels'. It is not that, but it is an achievement for a woman in her middle sixties who had many reasons to be saddened by life. It opens brilliantly rather in the manner a novel of Jane Austen's might open:

'There is Helen in the lime-walk,' said Mrs. Collingwood to her husband, as she looked out of the window. The slight figure of a young person in deep mourning appeared between the trees. 'How slowly she walks! She looks very unhappy!'
'Yes,' said Mr. Collingwood with a sigh, 'she is young to know sorrow, and to struggle with difficulties to which she is quite unsuited both by nature and by education, difficulties which no one could ever have foreseen. How changed are all her prospects!'

But soon the plot becomes ponderous, the writing stilted, the imposed moral values, inescapable. The old lady still drives herself on inexorably. But the reader if he wants to follow has to drive himself too. Her experience of life was too limited for these stories which she built up with relentless artificiality. A good example is *Ormond*. She wrote it with a forced speed to please her dying father. He, we are told, added his own passages. 'In my 74th year', he says, 'I had the satisfaction of seeing another work of my daughter's brought before the public.' Maria read him the first chapter in the carriage going to Pakenham Hall to see Lord Longford's bride. It was the last visit that Mr. Edgeworth paid anywhere. Yet here again despite all his family interest the style never touches the qualities of *Castle Rackrent*. Here is her description of Lady Annaly:

Lady Annaly was a woman of generous indignation, strong principles, and warm affections. Her rank, her high connexions, her high character, her having, from the time she was left a young and beautiful widow, devoted herself to the education and the interests of her children; her having persevered in her lofty course, superior to all the numerous temptations of love, vanity, or ambition, by which she was assailed; her long and able administration of a large property during the minority of her son; her subsequent graceful resignation of power; his affection, gratitude, and deference to his mother, which now continued to prolong her influence, and exemplify her precepts in every act of his own; altogether placed this lady high in public consideration—high as any individual could stand in a country, where national enthusiastic attachment is ever excited by certain noble qualities, congenial to the Irish nature.

A hundred years hence our Society will still be here. I hope there will still be a centenary lecture for Maria. How much of her work will survive, how much of it will be read in the intervening interval? Of this in all honesty I must register doubts. But one thing will remain, the image of Edgeworthstown, and of this extraordinary family. Their spirits undiminished by violence and revolution and war. They are undeterred by danger and discomfort. Out of time they shall not be touched by time but represent something much to be valued in the human spirit. I think, also, that her own love of Ireland will remain and the writing that came out of it and I will conclude with some of the last lines she wrote when she was 82.

Ireland with all thy faults, thy follies too
I love thee still: still with a candid eye must view
Thy wit, too quick, still blundering into sense
Thy reckless humour; sad improvidence,
And even what sober judges follies call
I, looking at the Heart, forget them all.

# DON CARLOS COLOMA MEMORIAL LECTURE

This lecture, in memory of Don Carlos Coloma, has been founded by the will of Dr. Olga Turner, Spanish scholar and historian, and Member of this Society for thirty years.

---

# JONATHAN SWIFT:
# A TERCENTENARY LECTURE

By MICHAEL FOOT, M.P.

*(Read 24 November 1967)*

*The Earl of Longford, P.C., in the Chair*

MR. CHAIRMAN and ladies and gentlemen, I think I should begin with a few apologies. Although, as the Chairman has kindly indicated, I am accustomed to addressing some other forms of assembly, this is almost the first lecture I have ever delivered in my life. There is also the fact that we have had, as the Chairman has indicated in another sense, quite a busy week. I had hoped that I would complete preparations for this lecture during the recent Parliamentary recess—what Jonathan Swift once called 'the lucid interval'. But unfortunately that was not possible.

It is a great honour to give the tercentenary lecture on Swift at the Royal Society of Literature. But I wish to make clear at the outset what will become even more apparent later—that I am only an amateur Swiftian. My own views about him are subject to perpetual variation. All that I offer now is an interim verdict, subject to the next scholarly discoveries, and in doing so I must pay tribute to the great Swiftian scholars, some of whom have died recently—to Harold Williams, Herbert Davis, and others and to many in the United States; indeed, so great is the bulk of Swiftian scholarship on the other side of the Atlantic at the present time that it must be a main contributory factor to the gap in our balance of payments My tribute is to those who have enabled me to change my opinions of Swift as I go along.

Nigel Dennis, himself a dedicated Swiftian, wrote in the

*Sunday Telegraph* last week: 'Every man his own Swift.' This truth was made especially evident to me when I went, earlier this year, to participate in the tercentenary celebrations for Jonathan Swift at Trinity College in Dublin, where he was educated. At the opening ceremony a Catholic Bishop claimed that Swift was almost a Catholic, which of course he was not; a Presbyterian Provost managed to conceal Swift's scarcely printable views about Presbyterianism; and the only speaker who lived up to Swift's standard of denying all hypocrisy was the President of the Irish Republic, about whom you, Mr. Chairman, have written with such charm and distinction. It was a remarkable occasion to see the President of the Irish Republic, almost blind, coming to the rostrum and putting the assembled worlds of scholarship and religion in their respective places. He explained his own difficulties in accepting Swift as a true Irish patriot. He described how the snatches of information which he had learned about Swift in his childhood had not originally been convincing, and how hard it was to suppose that any good thing could come out of such a stronghold of the English ascendancy as Trinity College, Dublin. But it was Swift's slogan which went to the heart of Mr. De Valera: 'Burn everything English, except their coal.' I suppose it was the most successful example of sanctions in history.

It is indeed necessary to go to Ireland to appreciate Swift. In England he is a great writer; in Ireland he is part of the folklore. You can walk beside St. Patrick's Cathedral and imagine, as Yeats said, that you see him round every corner, being cheered through the streets by the people, riding respectably in his carriage with Stella and Mrs. Dingley, or sneaking off to an assignation with Vanessa. In Dublin, for some twenty-five years during his lifetime, they lit bonfires to celebrate his birthday and I trust they will do the same next Thursday, by order of the President of the Irish Republic. It might be said that Swift was the first man to raise the green banner of that Republic.

I might add that when I returned from Dublin on this occasion I brought with me a copy of some of the latest essays on Swift which includes one with the title 'The Excremental Vision', dealing with a few of the more awkward aspects of Swift's writing. I was almost hoping that I would be stopped by a customs official so that I would be able to ask him if he knew what Swift had said on this matter; how he said that a nice man is one with nasty ideas. Alas, the opportunity did not arise.

However, let me return to Ireland later. First, I wish to present a few negative propositions about Swift. And first and most important of all, in view of the 250 years of slander which he has had to endure, let us understand that he was not a madman. Often this has been the charge. Often he has been treated as if he was a kind of inspired ogre, a devil touched with genius. The theory is convenient. It enables everyone to dismiss his ideas.

Altogether, the charge of madness has been made by the following, among others: Dr. Johnson, Walter Scott, Macaulay, Thackeray, Aldous Huxley, Yeats possibly, George Orwell, A. L. Rowse, and Malcolm Muggeridge, and that is only the short list. Of course, they all purloined the accusations from one another. My journalistic friends know that when a man gets labelled in his first press cutting the reputation will stay with him for the rest of his life. Something of the sort has happened to Swift. But about 200 years after his death, Oscar Wilde's father helped to discover the truth, and modern scholars and medical men have confirmed it. Most of his life Swift suffered from what they describe now as Bilateral Meniere's disease which accounted for his bursts of giddiness, vomiting, and deafness. Eventually he suffered from senile decay, as I dare say most of his accusers have or will. Swift thought that to be a most pitiful condition, but he was never mad. And even if it were accepted, for which, as I say, there is no basis, that in the last two or three years of his life his senile decay took on a form of madness, all the conclusions drawn from the suppositions are still invalid. For their is no justification here for any charge that he was mad when he wrote *Gulliver's Travels* some twenty years before. It has been said that a man's life is his whole life and not the last glimmering snuff of the candle. What some people have falsely thought to be Swift's condition in the last few years of his life is supposed to have accounted for the tenor of his writings twenty or thirty years earlier.

One of the additional reasons, incidentally, why some have thought him mad is that he built a mental hospital and wrote about it some of the most famous of his lines:

> He gave the little Wealth he had,
> To build a House for Fools and Mad.
> And shew'd by one Satyric Touch,
> No Nation needed it so much

He did indeed work and save for fifteen years to establish a hospital for the mentally deficient, which still exists in Dublin. That this should be taken as a proof of his own mental deficiency is a reflection on human churlishness which only a Swiftian satire could deal with adequately.

And, of course, once his claim to sanity is established and unchallengeable, his indictments against human cruelty and bestiality can no longer be scorned. The accusations against him of hardness and inhumanity are turned upside down. One of his contemporaries said: 'Nothing has an uglier look to us than reason when it is not on our side.' Maybe that is what has always stirred the paroxysms among the Swift haters.

I am sorry to have to say it, but the man more responsible than anybody for these perennial slanders against Swift was Dr. Johnson. I hope, Mr. Chairman, I have a most forgiving nature. I can conceivably forgive Dr. Johnson for saying that in *Gulliver's Travels* when once you have thought of the big men and the little men it is easy to do all the rest; I can forgive him, I suppose, for saying that Swift was deficient in both wit and humour; but what is unforgivable is that Johnson should have written of Swift in his last years as 'a driveller and show'.

Now the second charge we must dispose of properly, after these 300 years, the charge often accompanying that of madness, is that Swift was some form of sex maniac. Or at least it is suggested that he was impotent or syphilitic. All these suggestions arise in the age-old search for an explanation of his relationship with Stella and Vanessa. It is the seemingly inescapable conjectures about his treatment of Stella and Vanessa, not to mention those two more shadowy beauties, Varina and Betty Jones, which leave so sickening a taste on the palate. Biographers tend to divide themselves into Vanessa-ites and Stella-ites, and now, in the hands of Mrs. Le Brocquy, an assault is made upon him on behalf of Vanessa *and* Stella, a most formidable combination, and a heavy blow for a man to receive as a tercentenary birthday present.

I do not offer any solution to the Vanessa/Stella mystery— except the simplest; that is, that he loved them both and that his heart was torn between the two. The most plausible elaboration of this view, in my judgement—not proof, of course, because that will be never available—the most plausible elaboration of the view is supplied in Denis Johnston's *In Search of Swift*. I will not recite the complicated details. But if it is the fact, as he argues, that Swift was Stella's uncle and that he discovered this fact at some date that we do not know, then so much in his relationship with Stella is explained. It explains, for example, the extraordinary business whereby they were never known to meet in the same room and the terrible story of Swift demanding Stella's removal from the Deanery before she died. He could not live with Stella as man and wife, if those were the facts, without provoking or risking an intolerable scandal—intolerable for her as well as himself.

As for Vanessa, in Mr. Johnston's words: 'When cruelty was the only thing that could have saved her, he should have been cruel. She was wronged through the demonic pity that was the keystone of his character.' But that does not make him any form of sex maniac. Denis Johnston concludes: 'He was a perfectly normal man, of colossal proportions, motivated by two of the most universal, the most lovable and the most dangerous of all human emotions—Pride and Pity.'

Another familiar charge against him I must attempt to rebut. He spent a large part of his time—much more than a man of genius ought to waste—in seeking, scheming for, preferment in the Church, and that in turn meant toadying to politicians. It is, alas, true; this is what he did do, for a considerable part of his life. He devoted himself to becoming what he called that 'apt conjunction of lawn and black satin we entitle a Bishop'. He learnt the tricks and necessities of politicians in his own soul. In that world he noted that 'climbing is done in the same posture as creeping'.

Some people tend to deplore the whole of this part of his career, but I think quite wrongly. If he had never descended into Grub Street, *Gulliver' Traves ls* could never have been written. And not only in *Gulliver's Travels*, but in many of his writings, he offers excellent advice for the treatment of politicians. He said, when he wrote to Stella: 'If we let these Ministers pretend too much, there will be no governing them.' And yet, at the same time as he said that, he also wrote a great defence of Grub Street and the journalists, which I would like to quote at rather greater length. Maybe there are journals in this city at the present time, possibly *Private Eye*, which would find comfort in painting these words on their walls.

In the Attic Commonwealth, [he wrote] it was the privilege and birthright of every citizen and poet to rail aloud, and in public, or to expose upon the stage, by name any person they pleased, though of the greatest figure whether a Creon, an Hyperbolus, an Alcibiades, or a Demosthenes; but, on the other side, the least reflecting word let fall against the people in general, was immediately caught up, and

revenged upon the authors, however considerable for their quality
or merits. Whereas in England it is just the reverse of all this. Here
you may securely display your utmost rhetoric against mankind, in
the face of the world . . . And when you have done, the whole
audience, far from being offended, shall return you thanks, as a
deliverer of precious and useful truths. Nay, farther, it is but to
venture your lungs, and you may preach in Covent Garden against
foppery and fornication, and something else: against pride, and
dissimulation, and bribery, at Whitehall: you may expose rapine
and injustice in the Inns of Court Chapel: and in the city pulpit, be
as fierce as you please against avarice, hypocrisy and extortion. 'Tis
but a ball bandied to and fro, and every man carries a racket about
him, to strike it from himself, among the rest of the company. But,
on the other side, whoever should mistake the nature of things so far,
as to drop but a single hint in public, how such a one starved half the
fleet, and half poisoned the rest: how such a one, from a true
principle of love and honour, pays no debt but for wenches and
play; how such a one has got clap, and runs out of his estate; how
Paris, bribed by Juno and Venus, loth to defend either party, slept
out the whole cause on the bench; or how such an author makes
long speeches in the senate, with much thought, little sense, and to
no purpose; whoever, I say, should venture to be this particular,
must expect to be imprisoned for *scandalum magnatum*; to have
challenges sent him; to be sued for defamation; and to be brought
to the bar of the House of Commons'.

I do not believe that any better defence of the journalistic craft
has been written since that day.

But I must turn at last to an even more serious charge which
it is not possible to parry. And I introduce it in his own words:

> He was an Honest Man, I'll swear—
> Why, Sir, I differ from you there.
> For, I have heard another Story,
> He was a most confounded Tory.

It is true. Search as I may, it is impossible to refute it. He did
believe in a form of static society. He ranged himself against the
moderns. He sneered at scientists. And what he would have said
about the white-heat of the technological age passes comprehension. He believed that the hierarchical forms of society should be
left untouched. Walter Scott, certainly no advanced thinker
himself, talked of the antiquated and unpopular nature of Swift's
politics. Indeed he was inclined to curse all politics. He put his
verdict into the mouth of the King of Brodingnag. When
Gulliver was in Brodingnag, he explained to the King how
politics worked in England, and Swift wrote: 'The prejudices

of his education prevailed so far, that he could not forbear from taking me up in his right hand, and stroking me gently with the other, after an hearty fit of laughing, asked me, whether I were a Whig or a Tory.'

He was opposed to the idea of progress. He was inclined to be extremely pessimistic about human nature. Which brings me to the even more familiar charge: that he was a misanthrope; that he was anti-life; that *Gulliver's Travels*, and especially the last book, and the picture of the Yahoos is a vile satire on the whole human race; almost the most terrifying ever written. That is the charge which has been sustained over centuries. Before seeking to answer it I would like to try and pose the other side of the mystery.

If Swift was such a Tory, if he was so dedicated a champion of the doctrines of original sin, why has he commanded such interest and allegiance on the Left in British politics, and from the romantic revolutionaries of later times who believed in the perfectibility of man? It is no exaggeration to say that, for considerable periods since Swift's death, the protection of his reputation has rested almost entirely with people on the Left. Tories and Whigs have reviled him, Dr. Johnson, the greatest of the Tories, and Macaulay, if you like, the greatest of the Whigs. But the extreme radicals rallied to his defence. Before asking why they did it, let me substantiate the claim.

Swift's defence of the whole people of Ireland naturally made him the enemy of the English Establishment, and he became a great popular writer and a popular symbol. During Wilkes's fight on behalf of the free press against the King and the House of Commons, there were riots and political demonstrations throughout London. One of them occurred outside the Rose and Crown in Wapping, and it is recorded that an Irish voice above the tumult was heard to greet Wilkes thus: 'By Jasus, he's a liberty boy—like Dean Swift.'

Come a little later to the epoch of the French Revolution and its aftermath, when England was near revolution too. Evidence of how influential was the liberty boy is startling. William Godwin, father of English anarchism, and husband of Mary Wollstonecraft, mother of English feminism, was a devotee of *Gulliver's Travels*. So was Thomas Holcroft, tried in 1794 at the famous Treason Trial. When Burke denounced all would-be revolutionaries as the 'swinish multitude', a penny news-sheet was produced by Thomas Spence called *Pig's Meat*. It was stuffed with Swift. Whenever the editor had a hole to fill, more

Swift was used to plug it. When Leigh Hunt wanted a name for his radical newspaper, he called it after Swift's old paper *The Examiner*. And William Cobbett, as a boy, bought for threepence, a copy of *A Tale of a Tub* and kept it as his Bible. Swift has told us, he said, not to chop blocks with razors. Swift was Cobbett's tutor. Cobbett understood Swift's dictum which should be inscribed on the wall of every political journalist: 'Use the point of the pen, not the feather.'

It was people on the Left in English politics who came to the aid of Swift, when he was being attacked from quarters where he might have expected defence, and most significant and comprehensive was the defence of Swift against all comers by William Hazlitt. Across the gulf of time and politics there was a special kinship between their spirits.

In February 1818 Hazlitt gave a lecture at the Surrey Institution, just across Blackfriar's Bridge. There he defended Swift as a writer and a poet, and was even prepared to forgive him for having been a Tory. At that time when Jeffrey and Macaulay were unleashing their diatribes, Hazlitt's lecture begins to sound like the modern scholar's defence of *Gulliver's Travels*. He said: 'It is an attempt to tear off the mask of imposture from the world; and nothing but imposture has the right to complain of it.' Sitting in the audience and among the most appreciative was John Keats who specially marked Hazlitt's reference to Swift. From that day forward, the political lineage of those on the Left who have sought a similar inspiration in Swift comes up to modern times; through people like H. W. Nevinson to George Orwell. The orthodox, the established, the contented, the complacent have always been afraid to see Swift's books too widely distributed. They are right; *Gulliver's Travels* is a more revolutionary manual than the *Thoughts of Mao*.

Swift hated authoritarianism. He sometimes wrote in terms of a fierce, if primitive, class war between rich and poor, following his experiences of what he had seen in Ireland. He was bitterly anti-militarist. He is the greatest of all opponents of imperialism, of the attempt of one nation to impose its will upon another. Of course, he learnt this in Ireland. Stella too, to her honour, strongly shared his sympathy. All government without the consent of the governed, he said, is the very definition of slavery.

It is not surprising, then, that Hazlitt, Cobbett, Leigh Hunt, and the rest, in the midst of another great war, when spies and informers were at work in the interests of exorbitant authority, in the age of the press gang and Peterloo, treasured *Gulliver's Travels* as a seditious tract. It spoke the truth at that time called high treason. It sounded the trumpet of continued anarchistic revolt when others who did so were being deported to Botany Bay. It assailed the Establishment, Whig and Tory (what Cobbett called 'The Thing'), and reduced the whole bunch to their proper stature. Small wonder that stout patriots like Dr. Johnson, Scott, Macaulay, and the rest found the meat too strong for them. But they might have hit upon a more creditable retort than to call the man mad. Not even we today, in the twentieth century, regard a hatred of slavery, oppression, and war as infallible signs of insanity.

There is another strand in Swift which appeals to the Left, apart from these more obvious ones which I have cited. It may be illustrated by a digression. The book, in my opinion, which best refutes the charge of misanthropy against Swift is Miss Kathleen Williams's *Jonathan Swift and the Age of Compromise*. She shows that, when Swift described the Yahoos, he was not giving his view of the human race; nor was the country of the Houyhnhnms a description of his Utopia. To state the proposition with the utmost crudity, he was seeking to reconcile human beings to their condition and instructing them how they should behave towards one another. *Gulliver's Travels* ceases to be the outburst of a monster, but the considered, highly complex verdict of a luminous, compassionate mind.

During the course of the exposition, Miss Williams makes an astonishing comparison, between Swift and Montaigne. If Swift was really the hater of life and humanity, as he is so often portrayed, any such comparison would be impossible; for of course nobody has ever dreamt of making any similar charge against Montaigne. At first sight, or on first hearing, it may seem absurd that anybody should compare the meandering ruminations of Montaigne with the fierce polemical thrust of Swift. But the closer one looks, the stronger the case appears. Bolingbroke taunted Swift about 'your old prating friend Montaigne'. And there is another fact more clinching than any literary allusion. Swift gave a copy of Montaigne to Vanessa.

Once one begins to look beneath the surface several likenesses between the two emerge. Montaigne, like Swift, was a great opponent of cruelty, imperialism, and war—at a period when all these three were thought to be quite respectable—so different from our own times. The deeper one looks, the more instructive,

I believe, is the comparison, and the more surely it supplies the answer to those who have accused him of misanthropy. Swift was sceptical, like Montaigne. His scepticism never went so deep as Montaigne's. His pessimism about man and his sinful nature and the possibilities of improvement by human effort stayed close to that of orthodox Christianity, but it never reached the depth of black despair which is supposed to have resulted in his madness. Nor did it prevent him from declaiming, denouncing, preaching, and exhorting with all his skill and might, occupations which certainly would have been senseless if man's condition were incurable. No one indeed has ever lashed the brutalities and bestialities which men inflict upon one another with a greater intensity. He loathed cruelty. He was enraged by the attempts of the nation to impose its will on another. He exposed, as never before or since, the crimes committed in the name of a strutting, shouting patriotism. He had a horror of state tyranny and, as George Orwell has underlined, an uncanny presentiment of totalitarianism and all the torture it would brand on body and mind. Above all, he hated war, and the barbarisms it let loose.

War for him embraced all other forms of agony and wickedness. *Gulliver's Travels* is still the most powerful of pacifist pamphlets, and naturally it is these aspects of his iconoclasm which have won for him the persistent allegiance on the Left. Yet, I must acknowledge, the truth remains; that his general tone was conservative, that he eagerly resisted innovations, that he revered the past and seemed only to envisage or approve a society that never changed, and that the climax of his book is an attack on the deadly sin of pride, a sermon which Established Church and State are always inclined to applaud, since it helps to induce obedience. Humble revolutionaries rarely change anything. So, as I say, the hard impeachment cannot be denied. The fellow *was* a Tory. But he might have had some difficulty in selecting *any* party to join at the present time.

And that brings me to another subject on which I certainly would not wish to appear in any sense dogmatic—his religion. Most modern scholars insist, and they have substantial evidence on their side, that Swift's religious convictions cannot be questioned. They show that he was a most diligent parson. They show that he served the Anglican Church with a fighting spirit. Nobody can deny that. They show that he was careful not to reveal the evidence of his scepticism, if indeed he had it. I will not argue the case, but some of his contemporaries I also note were not so certain as some of the modern scholars. There was the famous rhyme, pinned to the door of St. Patrick's Cathedral when Swift arrived there:

> Look down, St. Patrick, look we pray,
> On thine own Church and Steeple.
> Convert the Dean on this great day
> Or else God help the People.

Despite the strong evidence to the contrary, I have never entirely abandoned the view that Swift wrote those lines himself.

He certainly did write what Yeats called the greatest epitaph a man ever had, and in that epitaph there is scarcely a tincture of Christianity. He was, for about two centuries, confidently consigned to hell-fire, but now, under the power of modern scholarship, he almost joins the angels. The Church has claimed him, but so did Voltaire. He was a Tory, but he gets my vote. He served human liberty. That was his own secular boast. He did, and he still does.

But he was much else besides. He was, after all, a comic genius, like Rabelais, Dickens, Charlie Chaplin, Groucho Marx, Spike Milligan; along with his other attributes he belonged to that company. He wrote two paragraphs in *Gulliver's Travels* which are almost my favourite of the lot, and which I beg leave to wind round my tongue again. 'He had been eight years upon a project', for he was talking of course of one of those scientists.

He had been eight years upon a project for extracting sunbeams out of cucumbers, which were to be put into vials hermetically sealed, and let out to warm the air in raw inclement summers. He told me, he did not doubt in eight years more, that he should be able to supply the Governor's garden with sunshine at a reasonable rate; but he complained that his stock was low, and entreated me to give him something as an encouragement to ingenuity, especially since this had been a very dear season for cucumbers.

Partly by this comic genius, he won converts in the most astonishing places. In her old age, when she was beyond the age of 80, the Duchess of Marlborough, once the victim of some of Swift's most savage attacks, sat up in bed reading *Gulliver's Travels* with tears of laughter and joy streaming down her face, and saying: 'If only he'd been on our side in the political battles of long ago, how much more easily we could have won.' There was Alexander Pope, who knew how to recognize a fellow master in the craft of invective.

The person I mean [he wrote] is Dr. Swift, a dignified clergyman, but one who, by his own confession, has composed more libels than sermons. If it be true, what I have heard often affirmed by innocent people, 'that too much wit is dangerous to salvation', this unfortunate gentleman must certainly be damned to all eternity.

Then there was, as I read quite recently again, Lytton Strachey.

'Such an undertaking', he said, that is to 'discuss the colossal mind of the great Dean of St. Patrick's.'

Such an undertaking would be no unworthy task for a Shakespeare. Less powerful spirits can only prostrate themselves in dumb worship, like Egyptian priests before the enormous effigies of their Gods.

or there is Stella's verdict.

> Long be the Day that gave you Birth
> Sacred to Friendship, Wit and Mirth;
> Late dying may you cast a Shred
> Of your rich Mantle o'er my Head;
> To bear with dignity my Sorrow
> One Day alone, then die Tomorrow.

Or finally, best of all, there is the unchallengeable lament of Hazlitt.

Oh when shall we have such another Rector of Laracor.

# THE MARIE STOPES MEMORIAL LECTURE

This lecture is in memory of Dr. Marie Carmichael Stopes, scientist and author, a Fellow of this Society from 1913 until 1958. She was an active friend and benefactor of the Society and this lecture has been founded in token of gratitude.

---

## POETRY IN MY TIME

*By* ROY FULLER, F.R.S.L.

(*Read 26 February 1968*)

*Richard Church, C.B.E., F.R.S.L., in the Chair*

NOTHING can be more depressing than a lecturer's disclaimers, but I feel I must start by saying what I conveyed to the Council when I was honoured by being asked to give the first of these annual memorial lectures. I have illusions about myself in other literary fields but I am not a critic. At various times I have been a reviewer, mainly of verse, but never without anguish—even more anguish than normally attends creativity—and a strong sense that my mind was too simple, too crude, to say what needed saying. Above all I have always lacked the power—and the will, if it comes to that—to systemize my critical opinions. Accordingly all I am offering here is an autobiographical and therefore fragmentary view of what has gone on in English poetry during the last forty years. So please forgive its deficiencies and its large use of the first person singular.

As I was about to prepare this lecture, I started reading the just-published letters of Wilfred Owen and was immediately struck by the provincial desolation in which this hero of modern poetry had to pass his intellectually formative years. In some sense every artist has to try to make the journey from the provinces to the metropolis, from the periphery to the centre, but in 1912 it was a subbornly hard one. Owen had no university grant, no paperbacks, no Radio 3, no record-lending library, no bright young men dominating the arts pages of the newspapers. At 18 or 19 his over-riding poetic influence was Keats, and even George Meredith he found unrewardingly crabbed. Had it not been for the accident of the First World War his development must have been greatly more difficult and prolonged.

1912 was the year of my birth. My life was as provincial, my background as non-literary, my schooling as uninspired, my further education as truncated, as Owen's. But at 16 I bought Ezra Pound's *Selected Poems*, then just published, edited and introduced by T. S. Eliot. And I knew the Eliot collected poems of 1925. Needless to say, such poetic education was completely extra-curricular, for at that time the verse anthologies included in the set books for matriculation took one no farther than Margaret L. Woods and John Drinkwater. In other words, I was lucky enough to come into the 'modern movement' in poetry after it had ceased to be a mere metropolitan secret but before it had become academic or historical, and, of course, long before questions of style had taken on the absurdities and evanescence of questions of fashion.

The Pound–Eliot revolution was just about as old as I was. In 1928 its subtleties, naturally enough, passed over my head. But the two things that struck me about the work of these two poets had the meat of the matter in them, in however primitive and undigested a form. In the first place the very content of Eliot's poetry seemed to me revolutionary. I do not mean entirely because of its use of what one had been brought up to think of as anti-poetic properties, like corsets or yellow soles of feet, or because his octosyllabic stanzas poked satire at the Church and finance. The whole procedure of writing in free forms, the elliptical narration, the indifference to making prose sense, seemed to echo and embody my adolescent protest at the conformities of middle-class life. And in the second place one saw— more particularly in the work of Pound—that free verse had somehow ceased to be freakish or precious; that one had to come to terms with it. Difficult in this matter to think oneself back to the late twenties, but it seems to me that right from the start one realized that the example of Pound's versification was going to be a botheration all one's life. The free verse of someone like Henley could be regarded as an interesting experiment, the free verse of Whitman as some cataclysm of nature, not likely to be repeated. But Pound's diction seemed to have rules though I could not discover them; it was like contemporary speech but far from arbitrary; and it could be used for 'poetic' purposes as well as ironic ones.

... in the home of the novelist
There is a satin-like bow on an harp.
You enter and pass hall after hall,
Conservatory follows conservatory,
Lilies lift their white symbolical cups,
Whence their symbolical pollen has been exerpted,
Near them I noticed an harp
And the blue satin ribbon,
And the copy of 'Hatha Yoga'
And the neat piles of unopened, unopening books,

And she spoke to me of the monarch,
And of the purity of her soul.

To play fair, I have taken this example from the *Selected Poems* of 1928, but Pound's remarkable ear could be demonstrated far more effectively through a poem Eliot left out from that volume and which I did not read till later, the *Homage to Sextus Propertius*. In Eliot's introduction to the 1928 *Selected Poems* I read more than two or three times the paragraphs about Pound's versification. They are in Eliot's best style as literary critic—carefully discriminatory, excitingly suggestive, overwhelmingly authoritative, and finally, as one goes back and reads them yet again, wholly tenacious of their secrets! No doubt my simple mind has always wished to rush to conclusions in literary matters where conclusions are perhaps never possible, but Eliot's distinguishing three kinds of free verse—that of the followers of Whitman, his own, and Pound's—his repetition of his solemn pronouncement that 'no *vers* is *libre* for the man who wants to do a good job', and his insistence on Pound's verse as speech, all this in those days tantalized me a great deal.

I do not know where the discovery of Eliot and Pound would have taken me under my own steam. I seem to think that in the year or so after leaving school—and I left in 1928 at 16—the pure line of poetry's progress was for me complicated by such baroque considerations as the work of the Sitwells, and in any case my ambitions then lay more in the direction of prose fiction. However, when I was 18 or 19 I met the critic John Davenport, whose premature death not long ago was all the more sad because he never managed to produce written work to match his extraordinary knowledge and powerful personality. His literary effect was, as in my own case, in the perishable realm of personal influence. His mother was the music hall artist Muriel George, and in 1930—or possibly 1931—he came to spend part of his university vacation in the northern seaside town where she was doing a summer season and where I then lived. Muriel George and I had a friend in common and one evening in her dressing-room I was introduced to John—already stout and formidable, already alarmingly well-read. He had just helped to edit *Cambridge Poetry 1929*, which contained verse by himself, John Lehmann, William Empson, and others. In subsequent meetings he told me about Auden's 1930 *Poems*, copies of the first edition of which at the published price of half a crown were still available. And about a poet who had not yet published a book but who was going to be good—Stephen Spender. It was even more characteristic of his discrimination and knowledge that he should also commend a poet of the previous generation who in fact only in the last year or two has come to have the width of recognition he deserves—Edgell Rickword. And another thing sticks in my mind from those brief early encounters with John Davenport. I happened to mention derisorily the official notion of 'modern' poetry that I had inherited, for some reason singling out James Elroy Flecker, though Flecker was really a poet I admired. Immediately and in his best block-busting manner John pointed out Flecker's undeniable virtues.

So it was that I came to see the tradition of English poetry not only as something that persisted into the times in which I was living but also as a process without breaks in any crude sense. This feeling of the availability of the tradition to the young practitioner was greatly enhanced when I started reading Auden, who of course right from the start drew on the resources of the most elaborate and exotic traditional verse forms. Some recent critics have discovered in this practice of the Auden school of poets a reaction against, a backsliding from, the modern movement inaugurated by Eliot and Pound. Further than that, it has been said that the reaction was something characteristically English—that is anti-demotic, insular, class-ridden. The argument has been sustained by contrasting the free verse written by another American, William Carlos Williams, and Williams's followers, not only with Auden-influenced poets here and in America but also with the English poets who became prominent in the fifties. There is no doubt that most serious poets of my time have believed with Gerard Manley Hopkins that the diction of poetry must have a close relationship to ordinary speech, 'that the poetic language of the age should be the current language heightened, to any degree heightened and unlike it, but not . . . an obsolete one'. Since people do not speak in verse there is a constant tension between this demand and the demands of metre and rhyme. Moreover, for most of the period I am dealing with, the audience for poetry has been small and specialized so that the bulk of the poetry written has tended to be subtle or complicated—poetry for the study. Such poetry is apt to neglect the speaking voice in its pursuit of the solution to other problems. However, a poetry that does not set its authors severe technical tasks is likely to be no poetry at all. It is significant that the great bad poets of the past, like McGonagall, were rotten craftsmen, and that the characteristic of modern amateur poetry is its free verse form—or formlessness. Most of the followers of William Carlos Williams seem to me to be simply lacking in skill—and this also applies to other *soi-disant* anti-establishment schools like the current 'Liverpool' poets. But this is not to say that traditional metre, in particular the iambic line, does not impose a tyranny which many poets feel they must resist to survive, and I would like to return to this subject later.

I have not mentioned yet the quality in Auden and the Audenesque poets of the thirties which brought out the strongest response from me—their political commitment. In one's youth the poetry of one's exact contemporaries is exciting in an almost indefinable way—tone of voice, revelations, shared problems posed and solved. This excitement was what I got first—from a poem of Spender's, for example, which appeared in the *Oxford Poetry* of 1930:

> My parents quarrel in the neighbour room:—
> 'How did you sleep last night?' 'I woke at four
> To hear the wind that sulks along the floor
> Blowing up dust like ashes from the tomb.'
>
> 'I was awake at three.' 'I heard the moth
> Breed perilous worms.' 'I wept
> All night, watching your rest.' 'I never slept
> Nor sleep at all.' Thus ghastly they speak, both.
>
> How can these sleep who eat upon their fear
> And watch their dreadful love fade as it grows?
> Their life flowers like an antique lovers' rose
> Set puff'd and spreading in the chemist's jar.
>
> I am your son, and from bad dreams arise.
> My sight is fixed with horror, as I pass
> Before the transitory glass
> And watch the fungus cover up my eyes.

But during the next year or two, as the crisis of the thirties sharpened, so did my own political interests, and I looked in poetry as much for content as for expression. One cannot emphasize too much the sense one had, during almost all this period, of poetry being as intimately connected with day-to-day life as economic forces and the actions of politicians. One sanction for this was found in the poetry of the First World War, particularly Wilfred Owen's requirements that poetry should sympathize with the oppressed, should be truthful, and should warn. Generations of poets since the thirties have lamented or noted their own absence of political conviction and consequent inability to write within a framework shared with and understood by their audience. It is true that much thirties poetry put itself in an attitude in which it was capable of appealing to a wider audience than could ever have been there for Eliot and Pound. And at various times it made direct and extraordinary efforts physically to capture that audience—for instance, by moving into the theatre and through less likely projects like choral declamation at political meetings. But, of course, poetry remained a minority art and its practitioners middle-class intellectuals with an upbringing and way of life which made participation in left-wing politics just as difficult as writing in some immediately comprehensible and universal way.

One of the most remarkable features of the period was this very business of acute critical discrimination accompanying, if not going hand in hand with, dissident ideology. Pound and Eliot had been outstanding critics as well as outstanding poets and the mark they made on the critical practice of the twenties was by no means forgotten in the thirties. Two other great critics arose: F. R. Leavis continued the high standards set by Edgell Rickword's magazine *The Calendar of Modern Letters* and found an ingenious moral basis for his criticism more flexible than the Marxism that drove Rickword himself to the periphery of literary affairs. William Empson's brilliant verbal analysis also had a substratum of ideas by no means counter to the *Zeitgeist* and saved his kind of criticism, certainly during the thirties, from any danger of lapsing into aridity and triviality. There were also two remarkable editors. Even in its most deeply politically committed issues John Lehmann's *New Writing* never lost its consciousness of literary quality—simply because its editor was tireless in combing the world for contributions and in personal encouragement of contributors he thought showed promise, as, early in 1937, he sought out and encouraged me, though with very little to go on, as I see now. Like many others I also owe a great debt to Geoffrey Grigson. This was incurred less through his taking a few early poems of mine for *New Verse* than for expressing a critical attitude in that magazine that I gladly embraced as my own. Grigson's positive side tends to get overlooked. He was a champion of Auden in the days when Auden still needed champions, and he brought forward excellent poets who followed on from Auden, like Kenneth Allott and Bernard Spencer. He drew attention to poets both of the past and present who were in danger of being overlooked, and above all he emphasized the detail of poetry, the strangeness of detail in poetry, the necessity for poets to observe. (At a later date he published two extraordinary anthologies, *The Romantics* and *Before the Romantics*, which illustrate the penetration of his taste.) His demolitions were carried out with sharpness and concision. Perhaps his major touchstones for bad work were sentimentality and pretentiousness, and I could not have agreed with him more, and still agree.

I see now—possibly I saw then—that in my case a puritan left-wing orthodoxy was carried too strictly into my verse. Much of what I wrote in the thirties was too stiff, too narrow, played an instrument of one note of middle-class doom, with an occasional harmonic squeak of hope for the proletariat. Only a few deeply felt pieces written by John Cornford during the Spanish Civil War successfully, it seems to me, versified the political ideals characteristic of the period. On the other hand, I think, looking back, that lack of talent rather than political commitment led to my unsuccess and that of several poets with my attitudes. For Christopher Caudwell, an undeviating member of the Communist Party, now stands out as one of the most remarkable poets of the time, though he was killed in Spain early in 1937 before he was 30, and his poetry was only part of a literary output that included fiction, literary criticism, and works of science. How the historical sense, a rationalist philosophy, a horror of oppression may inform poetry without choking poetry's need for fantasy and detail is shown by his poem 'Tierra del Fuego':

When our full-bosomed ship drave through the Straits,
Our eyeballs frozen with continual watch,
A Diego said: 'In those chill-swirling waters
What monsters move, rolling beneath our keel!'

And at his words the hoarse bird-bearing night
Blazed with sharp fires, in rank seraphic ranged,

An orderly regression of bright eyes
That watched us. Voiceless company of comets . . .

'An angel stands by each, tending with art
His steady flame, his curled brows bent in thought,
Ingeminating some creative hymn,'
So said our captain, in his gallery kneeling.

'With menial breach each puffs his fervour up,
And these will watch us till we fetch the point
And, wearing ship, stand for the north again.
Look that you keep your hearts and speeches clean.'

'No,' muttered our arquebusier in his beard,
'A devil, shapen like a rocky hill,
Gorged with the larded flesh of heretics,
Spirts out these touch-flares from his creviced hide.'

Dawn came. Landing, priest-guarded, for fresh water
We found some naked manlings, foul as monkeys,
Who shivered, squatting in their holes of filth,
And cast opprobrious rubbish; till we charged.

Mere brutes they knelt, revering Christian giants.
A few we spitted on our swords; the rest
Our priests whipped till they owned the Christ; one girl
Ape-faced but breasted well, our captain took.

With the coming of the long-anticipated war my poetry
certainly improved. The awkward division between middle-class
life and the action required to change it was swallowed up by
existence in the air raids and then by the general fate of being
called up for military service. The London of 1940 and 1941 has
recently been acutely characterized by Julian Symons (*The
London Magazine*, January 1968)—a city more nearly egalitarian than it has ever been in the last quarter of a century, is
one of his phrases for it. Life in the non-commissioned ranks of
the Royal Navy even more obviously sharpened one's senses
and absolved from the guilt of being cut off from the oppressed
masses. However, just as, in the way Symons has described, the
moment of truth passed for the civilian population, so the poetry
that in fact resulted from the service poets of the Second
World War was quite different from what might have been anti-
cipated. Of course, it was plain that they were to voice neither
Brookian heroics nor the pacifist anger and pity of Sassoon and
Owen. But since no military or political situation ever developed

in this country—as, for example, it did in France—to test the
allegiance of poets in a radical way, there was an anti-climatic
sense that the important things had all been said twenty-five years
before. On the one hand, there was the overwhelming conviction that after all England was fighting for the right side: on the
other, anything like Churchillian heroics were impossible since
the England was still the England of the National Government.
London's brief egalitarian atmosphere was an illusion reared
by dislocation, shared disasters, and impending invasion.

It is true that Alun Lewis began conscientiously as a poet in
the humanitarian tradition of the poets of the later stages of the
First World War. But how could the life of a soldier in training
and in camp—and a soldier whose childhood had been spent in
a period of social disillusion—how could such a life provide
similar objective correlatives to those of the trench warfare of
1914–18? Besides, Lewis proved to be essentially a poet of
organic development with an impelling need to dig into his
interior doubts and discriminations—as demonstrated by the
poetry he wrote when he left England for India. Keith Douglas
and Alan Ross, poets rather younger than Lewis, produced a
body of work that gave a vivid notion of what combat and its
aftermath was like. But neither in the field of technique nor
ideological penetration did the war poets much change the
state of English poetry.

One inevitably looks back on a period with too undifferenti-
ating an eye. Certainly the thirties now seems indubitably a
time in which poetry was written of remarkable diversity and
richness—from the spare anecdotes of Norman Cameron to the
surrealist rhetoric of David Gascoyne. But those of my own
persuasions who lived through the epoch were constantly nagged
by our consciousness of how far short our lives and work fell
from experiencing and interpreting the essential age. Nor were
we shy of criticizing the backslidings in this respect of those of
more talent and success. There was an acidulous gulf between
public-school communists and 'real' communists. Spender's
Marxism was diluted with liberalism: Day Lewis's was too
mechanically reflected in his poetry. And so forth. Such conflicts
and squabbles were important, though only their broad consequences can now be descried. The thirties poets may have
been 'committed' (in a manner extraordinary viewed from
another era) but they were not uniformly committed to a strong
political movement nor to a philosophy with clear views about
the relation of art to the artist's existence in society. In a variety

of ways and for a variety of reasons—which a novelist would
have been hard put to to invent—the war came and went
without involving most of the leading thirties poets, or at any
rate involving them as their fellow citizens were involved. The
poetry of wartime was thereby not so much impoverished as
diffused. As Ian Hamilton has recently shown in his discrimi-
nating and sympathetic anthology, *The Poetry of War 1939–1945*,
there was a line through the first half of the forties that continued the dominating tradition of the thirties—the tradition
that required the poet to relate to common speech, to observation, to life as it is lived. But at the same time there was incuba-
ting a curious regression to romantic themes, consciously poetic
language, and a critical eclecticism—a Muse of Georgian cast,
almost pre-Eliot and Pound. For example, Keith Douglas had
started as a boy by actually contributing to Grigson's *New Verse*,
but at Oxford encountered and for a time partly succumbed
to the new romanticism. Only during the North African
campaign did his language return whole-heartedly to the mus-
cularity of the early Auden.

The second half of the forties seems to me to have been most
characteristically of deplorable critical standards and of slap-
dash poetical practice. By now Auden was inescapably an
American poet; neither Grigson nor Julian Symons had returned
to the editorial chores of little poetry magazines; Alun Lewis
and Keith Douglas were dead. It was a period which saw the
end of John Lehmann's amazingly successful *Penguin New
Writing* and which his imaginative publishing firm did not long
survive. No doubt my view of this lustrum is not less jaundiced
on account of the personal difficulties I had in trying to make
poetry again out of a civilian life—difficulties that had already
appeared when in the Navy I had exchanged a seat in the
Petty Officers' Mess for a chair at the Admiralty. The mood is
not greatly exaggerated in a poem which I probably wrote late
in 1948. It appeared in the January 1949 issue of *Horizon*.

Once again the light refracted through the dusty crimson air
Leaves the spaces of the evening blurred and bare.
Bats that flicker round the edges of the square Victorian lawn
Symbolise the bourgeois souls from life withdrawn.

Now the nightingale arouses us upon the withered tree
With its disappointing, moving melody,
And against the chalky purple thrown by distant main-road arcs
Flow the tired suburban leaves like mouldy sparks.

Here the mower furred with grass like filings round a magnet's pole,
Teacups left for ants to make our fortunes droll;
While we sit and try to think that everything is not too late—
Sparrows sitting on the sad outfield of fate.

Once and only once we were in touch with brutal, bloody life
When we got in or kept out of global strife;
And in desert or in dockyard met our coarser fellow men,
Wielding friendly gun or scrubber, not our pen.

How we innocently thought that we should be alone no more,
Linked in death or revolution as in war.
How completely we have slipped into the same old world of cod,
Our companions Henry James or cats or God.

Waiting for the evening as the time of passion and of verse,
Vainly hoping that at both we shan't get worse:
While outside the demon scientists and rulers of the land
Pile the bombs like busy crabs pile balls of sand.

And the best that we can wish for is that still the moon will rise
Enigmatic, cracked and yellow to men's eyes,
And illuminate the manuscripts of poems that foretold
All the ruin and survival of the old.

A rather different view can be taken of this immediate post-war epoch, one I have much sympathy with, and which recently has been put with great feeling by Jack Lindsay in his *Meetings with Poets*, a book whose scope is scarcely indicated by its modest title. Lindsay sees the war, as waged by the British people, as more consciously anti-fascist; the war-time increase in the audience for the arts (which continued into the post-war period and is still evident to some extent) as indicative of a real cultural gain; and some of the possibilities of a poetry appealing to humanity at large rather than to an intellectual minority as having been actually realized by a few poets of the time. Where I would hardly differ from him is in his summing up of the present situation, which I will quote later, but I think I myself lost Lindsay's kind of revolutionary romanticism before the thirties were half-way through, and I seem to have been resigned most of my poetic life to the virtues of keeping one's powder dry rather than trying to fire the big guns. Nevertheless, one is tempted to ascribe the miniature size of even the best English poets who have emerged since the war to their inability to transcend the superficial preoccupations of their times, to be nourished by the issues that lie behind and often run contrary to mere fashion.

During the immediate post-war poetic decline, I certainly urged a return to Grigsonian standards of skill in versification, the purging of sentimentality and poeticisms, a common sense of content. And in due time all this was fulfilled by the best of the poets who had been born in the twenties. Merely to mention the names of D. J. Enright, Donald Davie, Philip Larkin, Elizabeth Jennings, Kingsley Amis, and John Wain is to make plain the force and extent of the intellectualism and sanity that returned to English poetry in the fifties. It would be churlish not to be grateful for this and other talent, and unfair to lump it together as though it had one aim. Enright, for example, has always seemed about to find the means of voicing a really profound social protest; Davie at one time hovered on the brink of a fresh approach to the problem in our age of the long poem. But as early as 1956 I find I was expressing reservations about the then younger poets. They were, I said (in *The London Magazine*, April 1956) themselves 'a little to blame for not becoming firmly identifiable. If conviction and experimentation are lacking, if there is a general consensus about form and subject, then one needs to have a first name like Kingsley to be easily distinguishable from the ruck.' The occasion for this facetiousness was a review of *The Less Deceived* by Philip Larkin, a poet I was then apt to confuse with Philip Oakes. It never occurred to me that this extremely well-written book, with its youthful charm and faint sentimentalities, would become the bible of the period and that one of the pieces in it, 'Church Going', would be quoted, analysed, and anthologized almost as though it were 'Gerontion' or 'Sailing to Byzantium'.

But beyond noting this lack of proportion in their publicists, I will make only one generalization about the 'Movement' poets of the fifties. It is that I feel that, once established, the neatness of their verse and the domesticity of their subjects—by no means evils in themselves—intensified the need to break away from the tyranny of the iambic line. In the end the very measure seemed to hold the threat of yet another poem about a small dead animal or the poet's infant offspring. Of course, some poets born a little later than those poets of the period I have mentioned made the break early—Charles Tomlinson was influenced by the short prose-like lines of the American school of Carlos Williams, Christopher Middleton by modern German poetic diction. But I leave to abler critics the delineation of the niceties of the situation. For myself I came late to abandoning the safety of the traditional forms authorized by Auden in the

thirties. My own reaction to the dominant mode of the fifties—
and my sense that I myself had been through the period in the
forties!—was on the one hand to set myself harder problems
in the traditional field and on the other to try to move beyond
domesticity through fictional situations, and historical and
mythological subjects. Thus I was led, for instance, to writing
twenty-one rondels about an imaginary love affair—the precise
number and form of the sequence called *Pierrot Lunaire* which
Schoenberg once set to music. It is rather comical that when an
interviewer asked me early in the sixties if Auden was a con-
tinuing influence on my verse, I said less so as I had developed
myself and as Auden's own development had made him a less
congenial poet. In that snap judgement I was thinking more of
the ideology of Auden's later poetry than of its technique, and
indeed I was slow in realizing how much the technique had
contributed to the content. I suppose Auden's admiration for the
distinguished American poet Marianne Moore dates from about
the time of his going to America just before the war. Her poetry
seemed as idiosyncratic and therefore as inimitable as that of,
say, E. E. Cummings. Its metric is based entirely on the count-
ing of syllables, though it often employs rhyme, and albeit in
Miss Moore's skilful hands and animated by her curious and
subtle mind this system works to produce a poetry of great
interest and effect, one might have thought it too far from the
tones of actual utterance to be viably adoptable generally.
However, to think any poet safe from Auden's assimilative
power is as foolish as imagining Velasquez safe from Picasso or
Tchaikovsky from Stravinsky. Auden's use of syllabic metre has
in practice been so copious as to warrant its general consumption.

Indeed, when one comes to employ it one sees that its
apparent arbitrariness and faint absurdity are really not so, for
since one works in lines of an odd number of syllables one is
working at what seems to be a logical extension of the problems
of the normal metrical English line. Behind the eleven-syllable
line, for example, is the ghost of the iambic pentameter, but the
constant intrusion of just one extra syllable removes the sense
there is about blank verse that its possibilities of variation have
already been exhausted, or at any rate discovered, by the great
practitioners of the past. Nor is one worried that the iambic
may accidentally result—and this is another differentiation from
another artificial artistic technique, twelve-tone composition,
where the older concord must be deliberately avoided, stipu-
lation which has always seemed to me a ludicrous indication

of that technique's inherent misconception. No doubt syllabics tend to impose too many merely arbitrary and feminine line-endings, but for the poet the practice provides a way into the composition of a poem or indeed the start of a poetic jag by freeing him from the preliminary need to hear his subject, his donnée, his initial observation or image, as song—or at least as the often elusive song of traditional metre. It has other incidental advantages—for instance, quotations from prose writers can be worked verbatim into the fabric of the poem. Can I read a recent example of my own work? It has an eleven-syllable line *and* a few quotations.

> All through the summer a visiting quartet—
> Father and daughter blackbird, pigeon, squirrel.
> Soft cluckings in the tree announce the blackbirds:
> First it was him, daring the dangerous sill;
> Later brought his Cordelia of the brood—
> She pouting and shivering, rather remote.
> Now in her nature like all other daughters
> She drives him off the grapes and bread I scatter.
> Slate-flat, slate-blue taffeta tail embraced by
> Matronly wings, grey marbled evenly grey,
> The pigeon drops draughtsmen on the terrace squares,
> Patrolling ceaselessly. And in the mornings,
> Anxious at the window, one hand clutched at heart,
> My chinless friend, with soil-crumbed neurotic nose,
> And tail a brush for cleaning babies' bottles—
> Disconcertingly like Sam or Sue Squirrel.
>
> This summer, too, I saw in J. B. Bury
> 'That mysterious prae-Aryan foreworld'—
> Not really understanding the phrase, dimly
> Conceiving a life before the oil-nurtured
> Legions, before the language of short, hard words,
> Before the death ships, the bronze, the chalk horses,
> Which now survives only as our consciousness
> Of the dotty element in our natures,
> Or as a tiny, round, thinly black-haired head
> Called to the colours from a cretin valley,
> Or as the unmemorialed existence
> To which we may be doomed.
>
>                    The quite senseless war
> Through summer days will run into winter days,
> The war that during my life has scarcely stopped.
> And the government that I elected, like
> All governments, whether elected by me
> Or not, will be powerless or uncaring.

How strange that in this sphere my desire should be
Always so different from the general will!

'There is no bridge between directional time
And timeless eternity,' wrote the gloomy
German; 'between the course of history and
The existence of a divine world order.'
Though far from belief in a divinity,
One sees indeed what he meant (and perhaps there
The translator was gravelled for the right word,
As one is oneself)—for certainly what may
Be conceived to be the principles ruling
The stuff that surrounds us, they have not to do
With bird-song, bird-love, the propulsion of metal
Into men. And what but the material
Can ever confront us, its open constants
Expressed on inevitably baffling clocks?

But I am thankful, on the whole, for this chance
To share in irrelevant events—being
In any case borne on to a species of
Significance by the drives of a motive
(No doubt falling far short of the eternal)
That will change my egotistic young blackbird
Next year to a care-worn mother. Take note, you
Gods, how my boyhood began with my father
Reading the news of the killing of young men;
How my adult body struggled with a mind
At odds with the task an unjust world imposed
And broke out in lesions that the mind despised.
Goethe said: 'The idea always appears
As a strange guest in actuality . . . The
Idea and common actuality
Must be kept strictly separate.' Very well:
Assign the business of being a poet
To an order of things entirely divine,
And the anguish to its historical material;
And accept the consolation (in Kafka's terms)
Of a wound that precisely fits the arrow.

But suppose the divinities relented,
Said: 'Your existence shall accord with our wills'—
Would our being prove even more frightening?
What would the creatures cry out at our windows,
Dark on a sky of furnace yellows: 'Join us
In the dumbness of utterly pure feeling,
To the forces that stretch you out over time

Surrender, and rejoice in the cellular
Mishaps that must bring about your extinction?'
And what if ourselves became divine, and fell
On the pitiful but attractive human,
Taking the temporary guise of a swan
Or a serpent: could we return to our more
Abstract designs untouched by the temporal;
Would we not afterwards try to get back those
Beautiful offspring, so mortal, so fated?

I have made these observations about syllabic verse not least because of the growth in the sixties of the idea of the poem more as a spoken than a written thing. Several factors have contributed to this—the perfection and cheapening of the slow-turning gramophone record, the transistor radio, the increasing literacy or semi-literacy of the young because of improved schooling, and, above all, a return to the conviction, as in the thirties and the first half of the forties, that the poet has some special message or warning about ordinary life. Poets have responded to this aural movement—I speak very broadly, of course—by simplifying the texture of their verse, and the first thing to go overboard in this process is the strict traditional forms, which usually have the effect of complicating and refining the meaning of poetry.

Poetry ideally tends to be inexhaustible, and in the printed poem poets have been able to add the inexhaustibility of meaning to the inexhaustibility of melody. But there is no doubt that however complex the poem and complete the printed tradition, poetic worth is proved, can be tested, by the poem being heard. This is curious but not incapable of analysis. For one thing the poet has composed it, to some degree at least, in his mouth or at any rate with the same apparatus he groans or mutters with. For another, poetry is not, like prose, entirely a discourse of meaning—the length of fortissimos, the plausibility of transitions, and so forth, have to be judged more by a process analogous to musical composition.

But in its search for a direct contact with a listening audience it would be a disaster if poetry threw away the gains of its long development in print. Besides, poetry composed as chopped-up prose or even in irregular iambics, however 'poetic' its imagery or logic, is more likely than not to be lousy, and one must be uneasy about the success of some English and American poets on the poetry-reading rounds, just as one is about the success of painters who have never learnt to draw. Perhaps syllabic

metres provide a suitable discipline for the verse which more
and more may find its audience among listeners rather than
readers—they tolerate a direct word order, they arrange themselves in paragraphs, and, as I have said, they are a good
adhesive for collage. Moreover, a return to traditional metrics
after a regimen of syllabics makes one conscious of the speech
tones still possible in the older procedure.

Or perhaps these general prescriptions and exhortations are
mainly in vain. When all is said, the criterion of success in
poetry is brain power—brain power allied at least to a dogged
alertness and integrity. What appealed to me above all about
Grigson's *New Verse* was its utter intolerance of the silly and of
the betrayers of ideals. No doubt these characteristics would
have been less effective if they had not been able to go hand in
hand with the positive creative achievements of Auden and the
Auden-influenced poets. Though of course there have been good
editors and periodicals since, we have had to wait until quite
recently for a little magazine with *New Verse*'s intelligence,
acerbity, and standards. Some may find in Ian Hamilton's *The
Review* a *Hamlet* with a strong Claudius but lacking the Prince
of Denmark, and I would agree that the editor has been able
to enlist excellent hatchet men to help his own demolition of
the phoney without ever finding enough new poetry fully to
exemplify his standards. But *The Review* and some of the young
poets and critics associated with it have given more ground for
confidence about English poetry than most fresh turns that have
occurred since the thirties.

For the achievements of the thirties were built on a site
cleared of rubbish by Edgell Rickword's *The Calendar* and similar
critical phenomena of the later twenties. The litter, both
cultural and ideological, is far worse today. (One has only to
think how fashionable and ineffective the *avant-garde* has
become—so lacking in possible impact on real life that it is not
only admitted to the art departments of semi-official media like
the B.B.C. and establishment organs like the heavier Sunday
press, but actually dominates them.) To quote again from Jack
Lindsay's book:

Everyone knows that the Welfare State, the American Way of
Life, or whatever one calls it, cannot last and is steadily piling up
some awful nemesis. Everyone knows that the judgment day is
nearing, a world-end pushbutton war or a furious chaos that
defies imagination. And so almost everyone wants to rush on without thought in the goodtime racket, the profitable rat-race, the

accumulation of gadgets and domineering things, or else to rationalise absurdity and disaster in artforms that draw on reality only enough to deaden and acclimatise people to a purposeless world.

But he goes on to say:

Yet many sections of the younger people, here as elsewhere, feel that the situation is hopelessly wrong, even if, comprehensively, they do not know what to do about it.

I would add, myself, that as the sixties end, though the response of the young is not yet political to a situation which above all else is political (as it has been throughout my lifetime) it is nearer so than at any moment since the war—and therefore, it seems to me, the more capable of requiring and initiating poetic order.

For just as painting is more than paint, the order of poetry is more than an order in itself: it is an order that must result from the poet experiencing reality as others experience it and seeing beyond that to a life possibly ideal but not utterly incapable of realization.

# DON CARLOS COLOMA MEMORIAL LECTURE

This lecture, in memory of Don Carlos Coloma, has
been founded by the will of Dr. Olga Turner, Spanish
scholar and historian, and Member of this Society for
thirty years.

---

# JANE AUSTEN AND THE ABYSS

## By L. P. HARTLEY, C.B.E., F.R.S.L.

*(Read 17 November 1966)*

*Professor Lord David Cecil, C.H., in the Chair*

WHEN the Royal Society of Literature did me the honour of
asking me to address them, I accepted without too much mis-
giving, for I remembered a saying which my father was fond of
quoting, and which he attributed, I believe mistakenly, to Lord
Melbourne, to the effect that 'every man has the ability to do a
job he has the ability to get'.

This consoling dictum sustained me for some time, but as
the zero hour drew nearer it began to lose its hold. Someone
said: 'Culture is the sediment of things forgotten.' If that is so,
no one could be more cultured than I am about Jane Austen.
But merely to have forgotten something is not enough; and
what could I possibly say about Jane Austen that has not been
said, and said better, before? The discouraging epigram, 'What
is true is not new, and what is new is not true', began to ring in
my ears. At last I consulted a friend who told me, 'Jane Austen
knew nothing about the Abyss.'

I pondered over this, and the question at once arose, what
exactly is the Abyss? How does one define it? The term was
vaguely familiar, but it was a modern conception and susceptible of more than one interpretation. If it was a collective Abyss,
the Abyss that the atom bomb has dug in our consciousness,
even whether we are aware of it or not, the threat of universal
extinction, then it was historically impossible for Jane Austen
to know about it. Such a threat was not implicit in the French
Revolution or the Napoleonic War. Careless readers have made
the sweeping assertion that Jane Austen never mentioned the

latter, which is quite untrue. There is a reference in *Persuasion* to Trafalgar, and to the action of San Domingo in 1806, and there are many other indirect allusions: the prize-money won by sailors—by Captain Wentworth, for instance. And even if she did tend to disregard it, the Napoleonic War was not the international catastrophe that the two world wars of our century have been, still less the catastrophe that a third world war would be. One cannot imagine a Duchess of Richmond giving a ball on the eve of the descent of the hydrogen bomb, supposing she had been given warning of it.

No, that kind of Abyss could not have been known to Jane Austen. It has been suggested that she had an intuition of coming calamity and for that very reason kept her pen and her thoughts away from it. I do not find this argument convincing, for the pen no less than the tongue goes to the sore place. But most of the Janeites I consulted said, 'Nonsense, of course she knew nothing about the Abyss, if there is one, and thank goodness she didn't. Thank goodness we can bask in the sunshine of her mind and the inspiration which commonsense and confidence in the social order helped to give her, without indulging in such dark preoccupations.'

But supposing the Abyss represented not a cosmic but a personal catastrophe? As far as I know Jane Austen only uses the word abyss once, when she puts it into the mouth of Henry Tilney, perhaps the most amiable and attractive of her heroes. Catherine Morland says that in Bath she sees a variety of people in every street but at home in the country she can only go and call on Mrs. Allen. Mr. Tilney, we are told, was much amused. 'Only go and call on Mrs. Allen!' he repeated. 'What a picture of intellectual poverty! However, when you sink into this abyss again, you will have more to say. You will be able to talk of Bath and of all that you did here.' So the Abyss was, for Henry Tilney, the intellectual void represented by a social call on Mrs. Allen.

But I think there are much stronger evidences of its existence in Jane Austen's novels, even if the word itself is not used. I first read them in 1913, when I was at school, and she at once became my favourite novelist. I preferred her immeasurably to Dickens. She wielded a much finer pen than he did; as regards style and construction, she was infinitely his superior; her characters were portraits, not caricatures, and the subtlety of her humour made his seem obvious and exaggerated. Her world was real to me, and his the world of make-believe. Not that I did not enjoy

Dickens, but I felt that he used his genius as a conjuror might, to create illusions, whereas she used hers to irradiate the unchanging surface and texture of life; by her selectiveness she enhanced its meaning and by her humour she banished its humdrumness. It was her humour that especially appealed to me, for I felt it was a kind of universal solvent, that could be applied to any experience and, by making it comic, would make it comprehensible and even enjoyable. One only had to look at things the Jane Austen way and all would be well. Life at a public school was not always easy or pleasant. I felt unconsciously that had Jane Austen chosen to describe it she could have made it a subject for comedy without romanticizing or distorting it, but simply by seeing its comic side, as she had seen the comic side of *The Mysteries of Udolpho*, whose terrors I could never take seriously after I had read *Northanger Abbey*. Public schools do not come much into Jane Austen's books—Eton and Westminster are mentioned—but I felt she would have understood them by her unrivalled knowledge of the strains and stresses of a stable and conventional society—and what more stable and conventional (as it seemed then) was there than public school life? It did not occur to me that Jane Austen who was self-educated, except for one year's schooling at the gatehouse of Reading Abbey, which ended when she was 9, would not have written a school story. I did not then know about the two inches of ivory to which she (perhaps mistakenly) confined herself. I thought that her attitude of mind—her prevailing sense of life as a subject for comedy—could be applied to any set of circumstances. I did not realize that it implied respect for certain social rules and regulations—for civilized living, in fact—and if she had doubted these values, moral and social, her exquisite art might have fluttered with a broken wing. As Blake said,

If the sun and moon should doubt,
They'd immediately go out,

and it is the same with the artist, if he loses his fundamental conviction.

The war came, and as Gunner Hartley I went into the army, which had its rules and regulations, indeed, but not such as I understood, nor do I think Jane Austen would have understood them, for civilized living had gone by the board. Although I never went overseas, army life did seem at the beginning a kind of Abyss; a chaos without signposts or landmarks, in which dread and bewilderment reigned. I think that during that time

my confidence in Jane Austen as an interpreter of life must
have been severely shaken, and though I read some escapist
literature, I did not return to her. Instead, I read *The Brothers
Karamazov* with intense excitement, for it seemed to show what
life was like in the raw—the kind of life into which I had been
pitchforked, although I never experienced its ultimate horrors.

After the war my taste in fiction inclined, or declined, to the
romantic. I returned to the Brontës, who had been an early
love of mine, and it was then that I read Charlotte Brontë's
letter to her publisher, W. S. Williams, dated 1850, about Jane
Austen. Had I read it before the First World War I should have
dismissed it with indignation or irritation or perhaps with a
smile, but in the light of my more recent experience it impressed
me deeply. I am sure that everyone knows it, but I will read
it again, for it puts Charlotte Brontë's case against Jane Austen
with incomparable force.

I have also read one of Miss Austen's works—*Emma*, read it with
interest and with just the degree of admiration which Miss Austen
herself would have thought sensible and suitable. Anything like
warmth or enthusiasm, anything energetic, poignant, heartfelt, is
utterly out of place in commending these works; all such demonstra-
tion the authoress would have met with a wellbred sneer, would have
calmly scorned as outré and extravagant. She does her business of
delineating the surface of the lives of genteel English people curiously
well. There is a Chinese fidelity, a miniature delicacy in the painting.
She ruffles her reader by nothing vehement, disturbs him by nothing
profound. The passions are perfectly unknown to her, she rejects
even a speaking acquaintance with that stormy sisterhood. Even to
the feelings she vouchsafes no more than an occasional graceful but
distant recognition—too frequent converse with them would ruffle
the smooth elegance of her progress. Her business is not half so
much with the human heart as with the human eyes, mouth, hands
and feet. What sees keenly, speaks aptly, moves flexibly, it suits her
to study; but what throbs fast and full, though hidden, what the
blood rushes through, what is the unseen seat of life and the sentient
target of death—this Miss Austen ignores. She no more, with her
mind's eye, beholds the heart of her race than each man, with
bodily vision, sees the heart in his heaving breast, Jane Austen was a
complete and most sensible lady, but a very incomplete and rather
insensible (not senseless) woman. If this is heresy, I cannot help it.

Well, this diatribe had a disturbing effect on me, as it may
have had on other devotees of Jane Austen, and it certainly
strengthens the case of those who think that she knew nothing
about the Abyss. But great novelists are apt to underrate each

other (did not Henry James speak of 'poor little Hardy'?) and to imagine that an intention that differs from their own must be misguided.

Writing to G. H. Lewes, in January 1848, Charlotte Brontë says:

> What a strange lecture comes next in your letter! You say I must familiarise my mind with the fact that Miss Austen is not a poetess, has no 'sentiment', you scornfully enclose the word in inverted commas, no eloquence, none of the ravishing enthusiasm of poetry! And then you add I must learn to acknowledge her as one of the greatest of artists, of the greatest painters of human characters, and one of the writers with the nicest sense of means to an end that ever lived—the last point only will I ever acknowledge.
> Can there be a great artist without poetry?

Charlotte Brontë was in her way a fair-minded woman; but she was critical and censorious, as witness the passage in her introduction to *Wuthering Heights*, in which she wonders if it is wise to create human beings like Heathcliff. Except for the Duke of Wellington, in whom she could find no fault, her armour of partisanship was by no means flawless.

In a letter to W. S. Williams she writes:

> I had a letter the other day announcing that a lady of some note, who had always determined that whenever she married, her husband should be the counterpart of Mr. Knightley in Miss Austen's *Emma* had now changed her mind, and vowed that she would either find the duplicate of Professor Emanuel (in *Villette*) or remain for ever single!

At another time she asked him,

> Whenever you send me a new supply of books, may I request that you will have the goodness to include one or two of Miss Austen's? I am asked if I have read them, and I excite amazement by replying in the negative. I have read none except *Pride and Prejudice*. Miss Martineau mentioned *Persuasion* as the best.

In January 1848 she wrote to G. H. Lewes:

> If ever I do write another book I think I will have nothing of what you call melodrama, I think so, but I am not sure. I think also, I will endeavour to follow the counsel which shines out of Miss Austen's 'mild eyes' 'to finish more and be more subdued'.
> Why do you like Miss Austen so very much? I am puzzled on that point. What induced you to say that you would have rather written *Pride and Prejudice* and *Tom Jones* than any of the Waverley novels?
> I had not seen *Pride and Prejudice* since I read that sentence of yours and then I got the book. And what did I find? An accurate,

daguerreotype portrait of a commonplace face; a carefully fenced, highly cultivated garden, with neat borders and delicate flowers, but no glance of a bright vivid physiognomy, no fresh air, no blue hill, no bonny beck.

Granted that any novelist, of lesser stature than Charlotte Brontë, would have been annoyed to be told to study the works of another novelist, especially another woman novelist, her verdict on Jane Austen's is still surprising.

Of some forgotten novelist of the day she writes that she is 'as shrewd as Miss Austen but not so shrewish'.

I think that the explanation must be that Charlotte had only read *Emma* and *Pride and Prejudice*, the two novels of Jane Austen in which the sunlight much exceeds the shadow. Had she read *Sense and Sensibility*, or *Mansfield Park*, or *Persuasion*, her opinion would surely have been different.

*Pride and Prejudice* and *Emma* are favourites with Jane Austen's readers, perhaps because in them she realizes most fully her gift for comedy and approaches most nearly to the perfection at which, as Flaubert did, she always aimed. Ske kept within her range of experience, or of the experience which she could best translate into art.

But rereading her novels after so many years, I rather wonder if this perfection has not been achieved at the expense of other qualities that would have jarred on or even imperilled it. Perfection is, one would think an absolute quality: there cannot be degrees of perfection. Yet no one would say that an object by Fabergé, however perfect, could be compared, in artistic value, to a painting by Rembrandt, however faulty. *Madame Bovary* is a great novel, one of the greatest and perhaps the most perfect: but its perfection depends on rigid exclusion of some of the most precious (and incidentally the commonest) human qualities. There is only one nice character (I apologize to the shade of Henry Tilney, who was justly critical of it, for using the word 'nice'), there is nothing in *Madame Bovary*, as Matthew Arnold said, to rejoice or console us. Perfect it may be, as a work of art, but it takes a one-sided view of life. And it might be argued that the perfection of *Emma* is partly due to the absence or at any rate the rare appearance, of anything that might not rejoice or console us.

> Faultily faultless, icily regular, splendidly null,
> Dead perfection, no more—

this is not true of *Emma*, whose life-enhancing qualities will never cease to delight, but it is a warning against the dangers of perfection—or the quest for it. I have been told, but do not vouch for its truth, that Persian rug-makers (those of the Mohammadan faith) always leave some part of the pattern flawed or incomplete, so as not to challenge comparison with Allah, in whom alone perfection lies. I do not say this to belittle *Emma*, the most perfect of Jane Austen's works (and, incidentally, the one most vulnerable to Charlotte Brontë's criticism), but as a plea for those that are sometimes considered less good, *Sense and Sensibility*, *Mansfield Park*, and *Persuasion*.

Revisiting the world of Jane Austen in 1965, I got a very different impression of it from the one I had in 1913. Then I rejoiced in the comedy; Mrs. Norris could not be too grasping and disagreeable, or Miss Bates too garrulous and fatuous, for me. I longed for their reappearances. Mrs. Charles Musgrove, in *Persuasion*, was another of my favourites, and her complaint that her sore throats were worse than other people's, has delighted me down the years, because I thought (perhaps with more reason than she had) that mine were worse too. The tribulation of the lovers (of the heroines, I should say, for they suffered much more than the heroes), I did not take very seriously, for I knew that all would come right for them in the end, and the social background I took for granted, as I took for granted the map of Europe; it had been, was, and always would be, just the same as Jane Austen painted it.

I reread the books with different feelings. They did not seem so funny as they had seemed. The change was not in Jane Austen, it was in me; my sense of humour had dwindled, and I could no longer see human life in the aspect of comedy. Nor, I think, am I alone in this. It is said that human nature does not change, but I think it does, and has, and not least in its sense of humour. I remember a friend of mine, a novelist, saying to me, 'There is no sort of joke now except a bad-taste joke', and she was no mean exponent of jokes of that kind. 'Sick' humour is the order of the day. Jane Austen was quite capable of sick humour; she had been condemned as unfeeling because of a joke in a letter to Cassandra about a miscarriage which anyone might have made if they had the wit to make it; and who would escape the charge of ill nature if it was founded on some malicious remark in a letter to a close relation?

But if I did not find Mrs. Norris and Miss Bates and Mr. Collins as funny as I once had, I marvelled anew at the cleverness, the subtlety, and the economy of means by which Jane

Austen makes her effects—the beauty of single sentences and the wonderful chapter-endings, which miraculously combine a faint note of finality with a stirring of expectation for what is to come. And I found many more instances than I expected to find of visual images and feeling for Nature—the 'March that was more like April', and so on. And if I could not look at Pemberley with the rapt excitement of Elizabeth Bennet, I could still see, with my mind's eye, what she saw. Those shrubberies! What a nostalgia they evoke! I should like to plant one myself, if my age and the size of my garden did not make the project what Jane Austen might have called 'imprudent'.

But what struck me the most (and this brings me back to the edge of the Abyss), is the sadness to be found in all the novels, except perhaps in *Emma*. There is more sunshine than shadow, of course, but there is more shadow than I remembered from my confident pre-war days. Many, many years ago an artist told me that every picture should have a passage in it 'as black as paint can make it'—otherwise (I suppose he meant), the colours would lose their relative value. I do not know if this rule still holds but it seemed to hold then. I studied a great many pictures, and always seemed to find a black patch somewhere. Indeed, I have seen a modern painting which was entirely black. Is the presence of a black spot essential to serious fiction?—for Jane Austen is a serious novelist. She cannot be likened, say, to Shakespeare or Thomas Hardy, without their tragedies. The two inches of ivory included much more than that.

As Lord David Cecil has said, there are no deaths, or deaths that matter, in her novels. (There are eight in *Wuthering Heights*.) What deaths there are have mostly taken place beforehand, and left only a legacy (sometimes a disappointing one) of money, to influence the story.

Money is discussed much more openly in Jane Austen's novels than it would be now. Mr. Rushworth had 12,000 pounds a year, Mr. Darcy 10,000, Mr. Bingley 4,000, and the Bennets, I think, a mere 2,000, which were anyhow entailed on Mr. Collins. Multiplied by ten, as I suppose they should be to bring them in line with the value of money today, and being more or less tax-free (though Jane Austen does once refer, I think, to some tax-problem), these figures represent a great deal of money and money plays a great part in the marriages of Jane Austen's heroines.

How was it that she herself never married? Someone, I think it was Miss Mitford, described her as a 'husband-hunting butterfly',

and she cannot have been a dull woman. We hear of attach-
ments to various men, Mr. Blackall (ominous name) was one,
but none which is properly authenticated, and both she and her
sister Cassandra died unmarried. The most obvious explanation
is that neither had a large enough dot to tempt a suitor, for
Jane Austen's father, who had seven (or was it eight?) children,
had, I think, only £750 a year to bring them up on and provide
for their futures.

Did Jane Austen really want to marry? All her novels are
about getting married, and marriage might be thought the
be-all and end-all of her heroines' existence; but as someone
has pointed out, despite this strong emphasis on the bliss of
getting married, there are few completely happy marriages in
Jane Austen's novels: Mr. Bennet certainly did not enjoy being
married to Mrs. Bennet.

'Oh dear, let him stand his chance and be taken in. It will do
just as well. Everybody is taken in at some period or other.'

'Not always in marriage, dear Mary'.

'In marriage especially. With all due respect to such of the present
company as chance to be married, my dear Mrs. Grant, there is not
one in a hundred of either sex who is not taken in when they marry.
Look where I will, I see that it is so'.

Perhaps Jane Austen, whose mind was so fully occupied with
other things, did distrust the married state; perhaps like Fanny
Price, she would not marry someone she did not love; but I
cannot help thinking that lack of money and the 'consequence'
that money brings, may have been at the bottom of it.

Why, otherwise, are there so many Cinderellas in the novels?
Fanny Price, Catherine Morland, even Elizabeth Bennet, are
handicapped, matrimonially and emotionally, by mixing with
people much better off than themselves. To be a man was a
great advantage; to be a rich man was a still greater advantage,
compared with the lot of the unmarried women. Not all novelists project themselves into their novels, but the majority do,
either from the wishful or fearful thinking which, more than
any other single factor, enables a novelist to unite his material
with his sensibility.

These heroines, then, or some of them, suffered from an
inferiority complex which made Elizabeth Bennet pert, Catherine Morland gauche, Fanny Price submissive, Anne Elliot resigned. It did not embitter them, however, still less did it make
them delinquents. I saw a case the other day in which some
teenage malefactor pleaded (I think successfully) in his defence

that as a child he had suffered tortures from a sense of social inferiority. Jane Austen would have thought this nonsense. A friend of mine said she lacked compassion—which is not true, she had plenty of compassion, and although she generally withheld it from evildoers, she sometimes extended it to them. Wickham gets off more lightly than he deserves, and as for that odious General Tilney! I cannot forgive Catherine Morland, or Henry Tilney, for forgiving him, on the grounds that his daughter's marriage to a peer had put him into a better temper.

On Jane Austen's monument in Winchester Cathedral (a favourite building with her, we are told) is quoted from the Book of Proverbs, 'In her mouth was the law of kindness.' Someone said that you cannot expect truth from a lapidary inscription and I think this one went rather far, as regards Jane Austen the author, if not as regards Jane Austen the woman. As an author she was not particularly kind, but she was just: justice is a quality that shines out of her works. She was a stern moralist—perhaps of all novelists the most moral. She makes it quite clear if she dislikes this or that character, but in company with Shakespeare, who put so many *bons mots* into the mouth of (say) Iago, she allows the most unpleasant or the most stupid of them to say a good thing now and then.

But I am wandering from my point, which was the element of sadness in several of Jane Austen's books. She did not write about Belsen and Buchenwald; she did not, like Dostoevsky, depict a human soul in the last stages of despair and dissolution, but she was acutely aware of suffering and sorrow; and sometimes, I think in portraying them, she overruns the two inches of ivory which was the limit she set herself. Suffering, of course, is relative; but how acutely one feels for Catherine Morland, so cruelly turned out of Northanger Abbey without the money to pay her fare. Catherine expected something horrid to happen at Northanger Abbey, and she finds it, though not in the guise she expected. With consummate skill Jane Austen plays on the reader's apprehensions, just as she plays on Catherine's; now allaying them with the discovery of a laundry-list, now renewing them with partial but disquieting revelations of her host's sinister nature; and when the catastrophe comes, it comes, as always in Jane Austen, with dramatic suddenness. The evil in Northanger Abbey was not a supernatural matter of cabinets and tapestries and long-forgotten documents. It was quite natural, a rather frightening middle-aged man, who caused her more suffering than any phantom would have. Of which of

Jane Austen's characters is it said, 'He is black, black, black'? I cannot remember, but how flat *Northanger Abbey* would be without this sudden irruption of blackness at the end.

'Happiness', Jane Austen is credited with saying, 'is a dull thing to write about.' For myself, in my later years, I find the darker passages often more satisfying than the social chit-chat, the Court Guide to Bath, the references to money, the importance of 'consequence' and 'precedence'—all of which were so well within her range that she could do them on her head, without always avoiding the danger of self-imitation. The irony which shimmers over her books is one of their most delightful qualities, but it can pall—it can suggest that we need take nothing seriously as long as we see it in the aspect of comedy; and no one, however vigilant his sense of humour, can see life like that, as if all experience was something that could be laughed or shrugged off. Charlotte Brontë's gibe, that Jane Austen ignored the 'unseen seat of life', is untenable; nearly all her characters (Lady Russell in *Persuasion* is one of the exceptions) are very much alive, even if it isn't the kind of life with which Charlotte Brontë had most sympathy. The charge of 'Nothing heartfelt' would be easier to sustain. I fancy that Jane Austen would have thought that to unbosom oneself to the public, even in a work of fiction, would be a breach of good manners. But there are times when she discards the mantle of irony—in the passage in *Northanger Abbey*, for instance, where she defends the novel against the charge of triviality. In this (though irony is present) she commits herself to what she is saying; we hear the true voice of feeling, the voice of personal conviction, as we hear it, still more clearly, in the famous conversation between Anne Elliot and Captain Harville, as to the relative fidelity, in emotional relationships, of men and women.

'God forbid', says Anne (and it is one of the few times when the word God is mentioned in Jane Austen's novels),

God forbid that I should undervalue the warm and faithful feelings of any of my fellow-creatures! I should deserve utter contempt if I dared to suppose that true attachment and constancy were known only by women. . . . All the privilege I claim for my own sex (it is not a very enviable one, you need not covet it) is that of loving longest when existence, or when hope, is gone.

With Jane Austen, almost less than with any other creative writer except Shakespeare, can one assume that her characters voice her own opinions; but one feels that Anne is speaking for Jane Austen here.

At the end of *Mansfield Park* occurs another, equally famous passage, and this time Jane Austen is speaking with her own voice. 'Let other pens dwell on guilt and misery. I quit such odious subjects as soon as I can, impatient to restore everybody, not greatly in fault themselves, to tolerable comfort, and to have done with all the rest.'

This is all very well, but Jane Austen's pen has been dwelling on guilt and misery for a great many pages, and prior to the Crawford episode there has been what Mr. R. W. Chapman has called the 'long-drawn agony of Fanny Price'.

That great black word miserable! . . . Her mind was all disorder. The past, present, future, everything was terrible. But her uncle's anger gave her the severest pain of all. Selfish and ungrateful! To have appeared so to him. She was miserable for ever. She had no one to take her part, to counsel, to speak for her. Her only friend was absent. He might have softened his father; but all, perhaps all, would think her selfish and ungrateful. She might have to endure the reproach again and again; she might hear it, or see it, or know it to exist, for ever, in every connection about her. She could not but feel some resentment against Mr. Crawford; yet, if he really loved her, and were unhappy too!—it was all wretchedness together.

Surely this passage gives us a glimpse of the Abyss, if it does not take us into the Abyss itself.

In its physical aspect Jane Austen's world was much safer than ours. There was very little danger to life and limb from accidental causes. Motor cars did not run over people; aeroplanes did not crash; and as far as I can remember, even horses did not run away. Yet there are moments when the outside world shows its teeth, and how vividly Jane Austen describes them! The Cobb at Lyme Regis: I have often negotiated those few unperilous steps, and wondered how Louisa Musgrove could have fallen down them, though I had no one to 'jump' me. Yet what a tremendous experience Jane Austen makes of it— just as she does of the incident of the gipsies in *Emma*, another irruption of the irrational and dangerous into Jane Austen's well-ordered world. Here was a group of juvenile delinquents, 'half a dozen children headed by a stout woman and a great boy, all clamorous and impertinent, in look though not absolutely in word'. Poor Harriet could not follow Miss Bickerton, 'who had given a great scream', because she suffered from cramp after dancing. Frank Churchill arrives in the nick of time to save her and escort her back to Hartfield, where she immediately fainted away.

The phenomenon of violence, so familiar to us, hardly came into Jane Austen's purview at all; but it is clear that she knew how to describe it when she wanted to. Her world was ruled by reason, by moral considerations; when anything goes wrong, it is somebody's fault; they have acted, to use a familiar phrase, without due care and attention—not to the dangers of the roads but to the dictates of prudence, reason, conscience, and religion —and for that they are punished.

Most people would agree with G. H. Lewes that her novels are deficient in poetry, though there is much more of it than she is given credit for. A more serious lack, I think, is that she makes almost no allowance for the irrationalism of much of human behaviour, an element of which we are only too painfully aware, and should be, even if Freud had not emphasized it, and perhaps encouraged it. Nor does she recognize the existence of evil as something to be reckoned with; there are a few villains in her novels, but few villainesses, except that very black one, Lady Susan, who might have come out of the pages of *Les Liaisons Dangereuses*, via *Clarissa Harlowe*, which we know Jane Austen read; or at any rate, we know that she bought it, for the bill exists. All the great novelists, except Jane Austen, have recognized the importance of the irrational as a factor in human behaviour, and the greatest of all, Cervantes, made it his subject; for what is *Don Quixote* but a study in unreason?

*Sense and Sensibility* is sometimes regarded as the least successful of Jane Austen's novels, but to me it is one of the most satisfying, simply because it does recognize, however distantly and disapprovingly, the force of unreason in human life. Marianne Dashwood is one of my favourite characters in fiction. I like her for herself (she was nice to her mother and had many other amiable qualities besides), and I like her because she does not act from prudential motives. She does not feel (in the beginning, at any rate) that money should be the *sine qua non* of marriage, or that love must be founded on esteem (an idea Jane Austen seems to have held, though it is, and always has been, unsupported by experience). 'I have never yet known', Mrs. Dashwood says, 'what it was to separate esteem from love.' It is generally thought that Jane Austen was on Elinor's side, the side of sense, against Marianne's side, the side of sensibility. But I wonder. Her mind may have condemned Marianne, but her feelings did not: Marianne, with all her faults, her disregard of public opinion, her antisocial tendencies (playing the piano whether other people wanted her to, or not), her determination

to go her own way and be herself—all these things endear her
to me. I cannot think that when Charlotte Brontë wrote the
letter about *Emma* she had read *Sense and Sensibility*. For surely
here the 'unseen seat of life' is defined as clearly as it ever can
be, and the 'sentient target of death' (though it never gets a
shot in the bull's-eye) is not ignored; it is present throughout
Marianne's illness, the wonderful account of which, with its
harrowing alternation of hope and fears, its complete lack of
sentimentality, its insistence on the medical and mental aspects
of the case, would give it a high place in any anthology of sick-
bed scenes.

In her last illness, Jane Austen was asked if she wanted
anything, and she replied 'Only death'. That was in 1817, a year
before the birth of Emily Brontë, who also died young and who
also, apparently, at the end wanted only death. As women,
and as novelists, the two might be thought the antitheses of each
other, the one loving society and the other solitude. Someone
said to me, 'If Jane Austen knew nothing about the Abyss, Emily
Brontë knew nothing about anything else.' The social background which meant so much to Jane Austen meant nothing
to Emily Brontë. Only Mr. Lockwood ever called at Wuthering
Heights, no one ever called at Thrushcross Grange, unless
Heathcliff can be regarded as a visitor, when he spent the night
in the garden knocking his head against a tree and howling like
an animal. The only concession, the only recognition, that
*Wuthering Heights* vouchsafes to society is when Catherine Earnshaw tells Nelly Dean that one reason for marrying Edgar
Linton is that she would then be the 'greatest woman of the
neighbourhood'. One has to laugh, for what neighbourhood,
in the social sense, was there round Wuthering Heights? Some
ghosts, no doubt. But all the same, there are many points of
resemblance between Marianne Dashwood and Catherine
Earnshaw, apart from the fact that the one nearly dies of love
and the other dies of it. Each was determined to be herself,
cost what it might to herself and those who loved her; many
of their remarks would, *mutatis mutandis*, be interchangeable.
Marianne recants, and apologizes to Elinor, to society, and to
God for her errors, whereas Catherine dies impenitent, only
asking Heathcliff for forgiveness. Yet they both hold our sympathy, or at least they hold mine, by each possessing a quality
of incorruptibility which can be summed up in one of Emily
Brontë's few recorded remarks, 'I want to be what God made
me.'

Catherine was not happy with her dull husband, Edgar Linton. Was Marianne likely to be happy with her dull husband, Colonel Brandon? He was fairly well off no doubt, but as Marianne (in her unregenerate stage) said to Elinor, 'What have wealth and grandeur to do with happiness?'

*Northanger Abbey* is a satire on one aspect of the Romantic Movement; *Sense and Sensibility* is a much more subtle and serious criticism of it. Even if we sometimes suspect that Jane Austen is trying to convince herself, she means to convince the reader.

To Emily Brontë as to Marianne, autumn was a season rich with romantic yearning. Emily shows it in a poem, Marianne in a conversation between herself and Elinor. Emily writes, as always, from the heart, and Jane Austen seems to make fun of Marianne's feelings—but they are none the less moving. The subject is falling leaves, and Emily's poem reads:

> Fall, leaves, fall; die, flowers, away;
> Lengthen night and shorten day.
> Every leaf speaks bliss to me
> Fluttering from the autumn tree.

> I shall smile when wreaths of snow
> Blossom where the rose should grow;
> I shall sing when night's decay
> Ushers in a drearier day.

'And how does dear, dear Norland look?' cried Marianne.

'Dear, dear Norland,' said Elinor, 'probably looks much as it always does at this time of year. The woods and walks thickly covered with dead leaves.'

'Oh!' cried Marianne, 'with what transporting sensations have I formerly seen them fall! How have I delighted, as I walked, to see them driven in showers about me by the wind! What feelings have they, the seasons, the air, altogether inspired! Now there is no one to regard them. They are seen only as a nuisance, swept hastily off, and driven as much as possible from the sight.'

'It is not everyone,' said Elinor, 'who has your passion for dead leaves.'

'No, my feelings are not often shared, not often understood, but sometimes they are.'

There is no doubt that Elinor gets the better of this encounter, but it is Marianne's words which, at any rate for me, linger longest, however exaggerated their sentiment may be.

I feel that Marianne was a tragic character and (with all respect) that *Sense and Sensibility* should have been a tragic novel. That Jane Austen could have made it one, had she wished, I have no doubt; the ingredients are all there, and she had nothing to do but change the emphasis at the end. The danger for a novelist of straying outside his range is really no greater, if in a different way, than when he sticks inside it. Who would have prophesied that Dickens would have made such a success of *A Tale of Two Cities*, a novel that was quite outside his ordinary beat? To experiment in fiction may be disastrous, but it may open up veins of imagination that the author did not know of.

But before I fail to prove my point that Jane Austen might have been a tragic novelist, may I quote a letter that I recently received on this very subject?

I found *Adam Bede* a tragic book, and poor Hetty Sorrell had all my sympathy, but *Sense and Sensibility* unearthed too vividly that awful period of desolation, rejection, and humiliation. . . . It is extraordinary. I have wept reading this book, and I thought my tears had dried up years ago.

# THE GIFF EDMONDS MEMORIAL LECTURE

This lecture is in memory of Nicholas Gifford Edmonds,
of the 2nd Black Watch, who was killed at Magersfontein on 11 December 1899. It was founded by his
sister, Miss Sophia Edmonds, a Member of this Society
from 1919 to 1945.

---

# WRITING ON ART

*By* JOHN POPE-HENNESSY, C.B.E., F.B.A., F.S.A., F.R.S.L.

*(Read 24 June 1966)*

*The Lord Butler, C.H., in the Chair*

I SHOULD begin by explaining the title of this lecture. The
term 'Writing on Art' embraces aesthetics and art history,
iconography and the sociology of style, art journalism and art
literature, lectures, monographs, and essays. I have used it
here because I want to speak not about any one of these cate-
gories of art writing, but about a factor which is common
to them all, the problem of transmitting what is seen through
the medium of the written word. 'Those who have eyes',
declares Valéry in his essay on Manet, 'know how irrelevant
words are to what they see', and it is a common experience of
people who visit picture galleries that the ocular impressions
they receive are far subtler and more diverse than the language
in which they are expressed. No one who writes about the
visual arts can long remain oblivious to the fact that what he
writes will be only the vaguest of approximations to what he
sees, and he continues to prosecute his thankless task in the
modest hope that his words may form a bridge between his
readers and the work of art that is discussed.

The problems inherent in art writing were present, and were
recognized as being present, from the start. Vasari, when he
prepared his *Lives* in the middle of the sixteenth century, was
aware of two of them, the need to provide a description of the
work of art which would establish its general character even
for those to whom it was unknown, and the need to reconstruct

and to explain the individual personality by which it was produced. He discharged the first duty with a fair measure of success—we bump along the runway but very seldom take off into the air—and he conceived the second in terms of narrative. But as we read his text we slowly become conscious of the presence, beneath his prosaic descriptions and conventional biographies, of critical values which enable him to co-ordinate the facts that he records in a coherent picture of the development of artistic aspirations and of the successive conquests of the human mind.

It is often said that art history is a recent importation in this country. I read an article a few weeks ago in the *Times Literary Supplement* which complained in effect of what disappointing figures English art historians were. It was followed by a reply. This was a new discipline, it said, and anyway middle-aged art historians in this country had what was conceived to be the disadvantage of having been self-taught. That in a sense is true. When I was a boy, and my parents were asked what I was going to be, they used to reply 'a *Kunstforscher*', and very foreign and exciting the prospect seemed. But in practice the hazards that face the art historian and almost all the weapons of which he can dispose are common to writers on art whose aim is not overtly historical, and in this broader context the tradition of art writing in English is not inferior, and in some respects has more to offer, than art writing in other tongues.

We are none of us, I hope, so simple minded as to think that when a passage from an art book reads well, it is good criticism, and when it reads badly, it is valueless. The qualification of the writer on art is that he can see, not that he can write. Claudel uses the phrase 'L'œuil écoute', and it is in that spirit that books on art should be approached. The most accomplished stylist is not necessarily the most deep searching interpreter. Perhaps I should take an example of the kind of case I have in mind. One of the best-known passages on art in English is the description of the *Mona Lisa* of Leonardo in Pater's *Renaissance*. I shall quote only enough to remind you of its general sense.

The presence, [writes Pater] that rose thus so strangely beside the waters, is expressive of what in the ways of a thousand years men had come to desire. . . . She is older than the rocks among which she sits; like the vampire, she has been dead many times and learned the secrets of the grave; and has been a diver in deep seas, and keeps their fallen day about her . . . and all this has been to her but the sound of lyres and flutes, and lives only in the delicacy with which it has moulded the changing lineaments, and tinged the eyelids and the hands.

That that is great writing is incontestible. Each time the *Mona Lisa* looks out at us from the pages of a book, Pater's sentences come to the surface of our minds, and each time they do so we recognize them as a literary accretion which is extraneous to the painting as a work of art. The second passage I want to quote deals with another work by Leonardo, the cartoon of the *Virgin and Child with St. Anne* in the National Gallery. It occurs in Berenson's *Drawings of the Florentine Painters*, and it reads like this:

One will scarcely find draped figures conceived in a more plastic fashion, unless one travels back through the centuries to those female figures that once sat together in the pediment of the Parthenon. In Italian art we shall discover nowhere a modelling at once so firm and so subtle, so delicate and so large as that of the Virgin's bust here. We should look in vain also for draperies which, while revealing to perfection the form and movement of the parts they cover, are yet treated so unacademically, are yet so much actual clothing that you can think away.

Beside the sublime cadences of Pater, this thought is awkwardly expressed. Yet it establishes almost to perfection the style of the cartoon, and without it we should look at Leonardo's work less perspicaciously. So in criticizing writing about art we have from the outset to apply a double standard, to consider the validity of the interpretation, and not just the fluency with which it is expressed.

Berenson—and I shall have more to say about his work in a moment or two—was a Janus-faced figure, part critic, part historian, whereas Pater, by his own avowal, was an 'aesthetic critic', an interpreter whose scaffolding of fact was supplied by other hands. The most successful of the essays in *The Renaissance*, that on Giorgione, was an afterthought; it appears, that is to say, in the second edition of the book; and was written in 1877 —six years after the issue of Crowe and Cavalcaselle's three-volume *History of Painting in North Italy*. In the essay on Giorgione, Pater refers more than once to the 'new Vasari' as he calls it, and it was indeed the 'new Vasari', with its resolute concentration upon fact, that led him to define his own interpretative role.

Although [he writes] the number of Giorgione's extant works has been thus limited by recent criticism, all is not done when the real and traditional elements in what concerns him have been discriminated; for, in what is connected with a great name, much that is not real is often very stimulating. For the aesthetic philosopher, therefore, over and above the real Giorgione and his authentic extant works, there remains the Giorgionesque also—an influence, a spirit or type in art, active in men as different as those to whom many of his supposed works are really assignable.

Pater was unfamiliar with the quintessential Giorgione, with the *Tempesta* in Venice which was then in the Palazzo Manfrin (he does indeed refer to a painting of the *Tempest*, but it is quite a different picture, by Paris Bordone, in the Accademia) as well as with the *Three Philosophers* in Vienna, but Pater then goes on to deduce the artistic personality of Giorgione from the scanty data that he had available, with a subtlety and sympathy and justice no later writer has equalled, far less surpassed.

The achievement of Crowe and Cavalcaselle none the less was very great, and I want here to strike out a claim for Crowe. The two men met for the first time in 1847, when Cavalcaselle was 27 and Crowe was 22, and between 1852 and 1885 they produced a series of major books, first *Early Flemish Painters*, a project that originated with Crowe, then the six-volume *History of Painting in Italy* and the three-volume *History of Painting in North Italy*, and finally monographs on the climactic artists to whom the histories lead up, Raphael and Titian. Both were dedicated men—their first joint book was produced against a background of physical privation—and from the 1870s on both were involved in other work, Crowe in consular posts in Germany which led to his appointment as commercial attaché for the whole of Europe, with one office in Paris and another in Berlin, and Cavalcaselle, in fine arts administration in Italy. Modern Italian critics feel a sort of proprietary right over the work that they produced. The attributions of the paintings, they say, were Cavalcaselle's, and Cavalcaselle was the only begetter of the books. The attributions were indeed Cavalcaselle's. That was admitted by Crowe, and transpires very clearly from the manuscripts. I was looking the other day at the notes they made of a visit to the Beaumont (later the Allendale) collection, where they studied the Giorgione *Nativity* which is now in Washington. There is a thumb-nail drawing of the picture, seemingly by Crowe, and also, in Crowe's handwriting, an attribution to a minor master, which was brusquely erased by Cavalcaselle and replaced with the name Giorgione. Cavalcaselle, likewise, was responsible for the astonishingly vivid colour notes. But once judgement had been passed it seems that Crowe took charge, and produced the far from undistinguished account of the picture that was printed in the book. Crowe wrote as an historian; his rather stolid style was rooted in nineteenth-century historical tradition, and he saw the development of the artists he described not as *Geistesgeschichte*, in what was to become the Viennese fashion, but as part of a firmly apprehended cultural and historical scene. Because of this the volumes on Titian and Raphael which he and Cavalcaselle published between eighty and ninety years ago are still the only worthwhile introductions to those artists.

But even Crowe was forced to recognize that at a certain point the paths of the historian and the art historian diverge. His books, of course, were written before the use of photographs became widespread, and when meagre illustration by means of line blocks was the general rule, and he had therefore, like Vasari, to shoulder the obligation to provide a literary account of paintings the reader had forgotten or perhaps had never seen, and to afford some indication of their style. The painting he discusses here is the so-called *Concert* by Giorgione and Titian in the Pitti Palace in Florence, which is also discussed in Pater's essay. Crowe's slow-moving sentences read like this:

In one of the simplest arrangements of half-length which it is possible to conceive, movement, gesture and expression tell an entire tale. A monk of the order of the Augustinians sits at a harpsichord with his fingers on the keys. The chord he strikes is true, for the two bystanders hear its vibration with silent complacency. It is probably that which they hoped to hear, for the monk turns, half-triumphantly, to ask, 'Is it not so?' His face and glance, the play of his features are all enquiry; the bald, bare-headed clerk behind touches the shoulders of the monk, grasps the handle of his viol and assents. To the left a younger man in long hair and plumed hat gives token of pleasure and acquiescence. The motive, thought and purpose of the story are concentrated on the player at the harpsichord; on him the light is thrown—a clear, sparkling but subdued light, such as we see within the walls of Italian palaces. His hood and cowl are black, his frock a shade of black; and the delicate opal of his aristocratic but muscular hand is relieved on a furred sleeve interposed to prevent a violent contrast. The subtlety with which the tones are broken is extreme, but the soberness of the general intonation is magical. Parsimonious impast and slight glazes are not incompatible with velvet surface and tender atmosphere.

The technique is enumerative and the language drab, but the paragraph effectively describes not the content of the painting only, but its facture and tonality. Pater's description of the painting is shorter and more generalized:

The Concert in the Pitti Palace, in which a monk with cowl and
tonsure touches the keys of a harpsichord, while a clerk behind
grasps the handle of a viol, and a third, with cap and plume, seems
to wait on the true interval to sing, is undoubtedly Giorgione's. The
outline of the lifted finger, the trace of the plume, the very threads
of the fine linen, which fasten themselves on the memory, in the
moment before they are lost altogether in that calm unearthly glow,
the skill which has caught the waves of wandering sound, and fixed
them for ever on the lips and hands—these are indeed the master's
own.

Pater disposes of the richer repertory of language, and his use
of rhythm and assonance is more sophisticated, but when one
stands before the painting, and I can speak only for myself
in this, it is Crowe's account not Pater's that one recalls.

In Crowe's last books, the volumes on Titian and Raphael,
the writing becomes a good deal more ambitious and much more
eloquent than the passage I have quoted here, and in Pater's
last essay on Italian painting, the account of painting in Brescia
and Lombardy that was printed in *Miscellaneous Studies* in 1895,
the standpoint is less unhistorical. But the question inevitably
posed itself of whether the two standpoints could not be
reconciled. Was it not possible to produce a book in which the
framework of fact was comprehensive and correct but where the
writer at a certain point shed his disguise as an historian and
emerged as an interpreter? In the 1890s there appeared two
monographs in which that attempt was made. One of them
was published in 1899 and was written by the 33-year-old
Roger Fry; it dealt with Giovanni Bellini. In the Fry canon it is
not a book that is held in particularly high regard. Virginia
Woolf complains that 'it seems to the ordinary reader at least
less vigorous and characteristic than the articles that were
dashed off simultaneously. It is a little elaborate and literary,
as if he were still in thrall to the literary associations of pictures.'
But since the pictures about which Fry was writing were, under
one aspect, literary, that was no reason for reproach. Perhaps
this criticism reflects some reservation of Fry's own. At all events
when the fine article on Giotto, which he printed in the *Monthly
Review* for 1901, was reprinted in 1920 in *Vision and Design*, he
found it necessary to explain that it was

at variance with the more recent expression of my aesthetic ideas.
It will be seen that great emphasis is laid on Giotto's expression of
the dramatic idea of his pictures. I still think this is perfectly true

as far as it goes. Where I should be inclined to disagree is that there underlies this article a tacit assumption not only that the dramatic idea may have inspired the artist to the creation of his form, but that the value of the form for us is bound up with our recognition of the dramatic idea.

Before he was committed to predominantly formal analysis, however, Fry wrote about the painting of the past with incomparable sensibility, and seldom were his gifts used to such advantage as in the Bellini monograph. How often do we not recall Fry's apostrophe of 'Bellini's intimate Wordsworthian feeling for the moods of wild nature.' 'It is only', he writes of the great painting in San Giovanni Crisostormo in Venice, 'in the landscape art of the beginning of the present century (the book, I must remind you, was written in 1899) that we can find a scene thus entirely modulated to the dominant key of a sunset light.' As for the exaltation one feels in revisiting the *Baptism of Christ* by Bellini at Vincenza and the altar-piece at Pesaro, most of it derives from the genius of Bellini, but there is as well a little bonus from Roger Fry.

I once said to Bernard Berenson how good I thought Fry's book. 'Of course, my dear,' he replied, 'I wrote it.' I do not for a moment think he did, but its spirit is profoundly Berensonian, and conforms to that of the much more adventurous book about Lorenzo Lotto that Berenson had published four years before, in 1895. There are some books that appear in retrospect to have been so thoroughly original that it is hard to explain why they failed to change the class of writing to which they belong. Carlyle's *Life of Sterling* is one of them; why did it not reform the whole art of biography? Another, in its more limited field, is Berenson's *Lotto*. It was subtitled, *An Essay in constructive Art Criticism*, and its enduring interest is due to the criticism it contains, not to the art history. It begins with what was planned as exposé (and now reads as an exposure) of Morellian method —hand is compared with hand, and nose with nose, and ear with ear—but slowly the light at the end of the tunnel becomes visible, and the book ends with one of the most brilliant reconstructions of an artist's motives and temperament that has ever been produced. Berenson at this time acknowledged a debt to Pater, but his *Lotto* is not Pateresque. It describes not just the artistic personality, that part of the artist's mind which was consciously concerned with the making of works of art, but the human personality which governed the imagist and directed the interpreter. The account of Lotto's religious paintings springs from the same world as William James's *Varieties of Religious Experience*. The alternation of close factual analysis and free portrayal of the artist in his creative role is found again in the most important of Berenson's books, the *Drawings of the Florentine Painters*. I call it the most important of the books because it is the one in which Berenson concentrates most fixedly on the process of artistic production and is least concerned with the spectator's response.

Late in life Berenson disavowed this book. 'I have', he said, 'regarded the undertaking of this task as a wrong turn in my career.' The reason for that was that his interest had shifted from the producer to the consumer of works of art, and that already in the second instalment of the book that was eventually to be issued as *Italian Painters of the Renaissance*, he had filled out the historical skeleton with a component of aesthetic theory. The vital change occurred between 1894, the year of publication of *The Venetian Painters of the Renaissance*, and 1896, when the Florentine volume with its exposition of the theory of tactile values came from the press. The *Venetian Painters* is a rather weak book, in which the ideas derive from Burckhardt and the language is Pateresque. Its successor, the *Florentine Painters*, is an altogether tougher proposition, and is indeed one of those rare books that seem on each re-reading to become more and not less difficult. As the series continued, with the *Central Italian Painters* of 1897 and the *North Italian Painters* of ten years later, an aesthetic theory was slowly unrolled. The volumes had a dual function, to inform and to explain, at once to formulate and justify judgements of value on the material that was reviewed. The fact that they are widely read is to-day due to the sometimes brilliant characterization of the artists described in them rather than to the residuum of theory they contain. But to the writer the theory was all important, and when in 1949 he published his *Sketch for a Self-Portrait* some of its most revealing pages were filled with self-reproach at the inadequacy with which the doctrine was exposed.

Surely [says Berenson] I could have learned to write? I do not refer only to the choice of words, to the images, to rhythm, to knowing where to supply the purple patch. Where I fall down utterly is in not knowing how to arrange and develop what I wanted to communicate.

Though this passage is exaggerated, it contains a measure of truth, as can be seen from the late book, *Aesthetics and History*, in which Berenson endeavoured to articulate 'the assumptions and convictions that have shaped and directed my work'.

The aesthetic propositions in these books were peculiar to Berenson, but the urge to preach is symptomatic of a tendency that appears in English art writing both of an earlier and a later time. The virus struck Ruskin when he was comparatively young, and as he aged the impact of ethics on his interpretative thinking became increasingly pronounced.

But what [he asks in a horrifying passage at the beginning of *Giotto and his Works in Padua*] what, it may be said by the reader, is the use of the works of Giotto to us? They may indeed have been wonderful for their time and of infinite use in that time, but since after Giotto came Leonardo and Correggio . . . why should we fret ourselves to dig down to the root of the tree when we may at once enjoy its fruit and foliage? I answer first that in all things relating to the human intellect, it is a great thing to have hold of the root, for it often happens that the root is wholesome when the leaves, however fair, are poisonous . . . and in the second place we ought to measure the value of art less by its executive than by its moral power. Giotto was not indeed one of the most accomplished painters, but he was one of the greatest men who ever lived.

The urge to spread the gospel of aesthetics not of ethics also overcame Fry, and comparatively recently it has attacked one of our most distinguished students of Renaissance iconography who has succumbed to the temptation to address us on *Art and Anarchy*. I speak with a certain lack of sympathy about all this, not because these books do harm, but because they were produced at the cost of other work. If Berenson had continued to function as an art historian, not as a philosopher, and if Fry had produced the books predicated in his early essays, how much richer our understanding of art would be. I am not advocating that ideas should be expunged from books on art; no one can look at works of art for long without forming value judgements, which he is entitled to express. But woe betide the writer for whom the ideas to which works of art give rise bulk larger than the works of art themselves.

If a statement of enduring value is to be made about a work of art, it can only be formulated from the work of art in the original. Before the use of photographs became widespread there was indeed no practical alternative. When John Addington Symonds published the volume dealing with the fine arts in his *Renaissance in Italy* in 1877, he declared in the preface:

I am not aware of having mentioned any important building, statue or picture which I have not had the opportunity of studying. What I have written in this volume about the monuments of Italian art has always been first noted face to face with the originals, and afterwards corrected, modified or confirmed in the course of subsequent journeys to Italy.

Symonds was not a particularly keen observer, but the discipline ensured that his descriptions were more animated and more vivid than they would otherwise have been. Ruskin, in the account of Tintoretto's paintings at San Rocco that appears in the Venetian index to *Stones of Venice*, restricts himself to those parts of the paintings which the unaided eye could penetrate. He describes, with great precision, all that he can see, and then we come upon the entry:

> *Cattle Piece.* I can give no other name for this picture whose subject I can neither guess nor discover, the picture being in the dark and the guidebooks leaving me in the same position. It is too high, too much faded and too much in the dark to be made out.

People who write on works of art still study them in the original, of course—at least one hopes they do—but I doubt if they study them with quite the same intensity. I am conscious of the difference between the way in which one looks at pictures now, when five or six or seven villages in Tuscany can be visited in an afternoon, and the way one looked at them thirty years ago spending half a day in each. There is a still greater difference between that and the way Ruskin in the middle of the last century imbibed long draughts of Tintoretto. Nowadays it is extremely difficult to form an impression of a work of art that is not contaminated or confused by an image formed from photographs. Anyone who feels the least interest in art can become familiar, at a very early stage, with a vast range of black and white and colour photographs of paintings, none of which he has seen in the original, and his response to the work of art when he encounters it is often just a little stale and tentative. Symptomatic of this tendency are the writings of Malraux, which hinge on a succession of photographic images. It is comforting to feel that anybody who disburses a small sum at a bookstall in the underground can become acquainted with the facts about Pontormo or Lely or Jan Steen. But as an art historian I would readily forgo some of this popular art history if these inquiring minds could instead be taught to look.

To look not only at works of art, but at the real world as well, in the recognition that for centuries the picture was a distillation of what had been before the painter's eyes. In that field the observant professional writer has an advantage on the art critic.

We are still awaiting the books about Dutch painting that are postulated in a few scattered sentences of Proust, and no modern account of a Dutch landscape can equal Hazlitt's of the great Cuyp at Dulwich,

woven of ethereal hues. A soft mist is on it, a veil of subtle air. The tender green of the valleys beyond the gleaming lake, the purple light of the hills, have an effect like the down on an unripe nectarine. You may lay your finger on the canvas, but miles of dewy vapour and sunshine are between you and the objects you survey.

Ruskin declares in *Modern Painters* that 'the man who can see all the greys, reds and purples in a peach will paint the peach right roundly; but the man who has only studied its roundness will not see its purples and greys'. In Roger Fry's *Cézanne*, where the form of paintings is analysed with unfailing perspicacity, the colour descriptions have the character of afterthoughts. Ruskin himself could bring such descriptions off to perfection, more often in the notebooks than in his printed works. How finely judged, for instance, are his notes on Poussin's *Triumph of Flora* in the Louvre,

with a sky as blue as a gentian, and massy white clouds, pure as snow; and a burning distance, all orange gold, as if all summer and autumn were gathered into one sunset over deep, deep blue hills, varried down by fiery flakes among the figures; the trees filling all the blue sky with stars of blossom, and the figures one bright unrestrainable riot of pure delight. One might think the spring wind had turned a drift of loose leaves into living creatures.

Then Ruskin adds this:

I forgot that the figures which come and go against the sunlight in this picture increase its heat in a glorious way; they have red dresses or fragments of dress and their limbs are burning orange red—half sunshine, half bronzed flesh. As an example of increase of warmth of colour by sympathy into one flash, it would be difficult to match it.

Much contemporary writing about art deals with literary content and not style. I do not want to seem to speak against iconographical research as such. At the magical touch of Panofsky it has opened new vistas to us all. But when one is expected to follow some writer's speculation as to whether the goldfinch in Raphael's *Madonna of the Goldfinch* was intended as a symbol of the Resurrection or as a prophylactic against plague, or as both simultaneously, and when one finds the Medici Chapel in Florence shrouded in Neoplatonic haze, one may well feel some nostalgia for the more simple-minded period when Richard Jefferies, in *The Story of my Heart*, could communicate with the life force from a wooden bench opposite Titian's *Bacchus and Ariadne* in the National Gallery, and when Symonds could write of that iconographical connundrum, Botticelli's *Mars and Venus*:

The face and attitude of that unseductive Venus, wide awake and melancholy, opposite her snoring lover, seems to symbolise the indignities which women may have to endure from insolent and sottish boys with only youth to recommend them.

We are left to conjecture whether Botticelli designed his composition for an allegory of intemperance, the so-called Venus typifying some moral quality.

Professionalism is not the only factor that makes writing on art today much harder than it was for Symonds or Ruskin or Crowe. Another is the sheer quantity of words that have been spilled over works of art. Poussin's *Triumph of Flora*, the Scuola di San Rocco, the *Allendale Nativity*, have been discussed again and again. What, the critic says to himself, can I say about them that has not been said before? In my experience as soon as that question is asked, the answer is condemned to insignificance; it will be peripheral, a kind of gloss on earlier commentaries, or distorted, or plain incorrect. For the test of what is written is not independence of earlier writers, but its relevance to the work of art. It needs a great effort of will to read the whole bibliography of a great artist, say of Michelangelo, and then forget it, go back to the works themselves, and start afresh. But that is the only possible procedure, and it is surprising how often the results it yields prove new.

The method of approach that writers on art adopt is to some extent contingent on the public that they address. In so far as we can speak of a tradition in art writing in English in the last hundred years, the thread of continuity is supplied by the breadth of its appeal. In that it differs from art writing in Germany, much of it excellent of course, but seemingly inspired by the conviction that the summit should be capped with cloud, and in Italy, where the best criticism, and very good it is, is more arcane and intellectual. I believe myself that most of the things that are worth saying about art can be said in an intelligible way, and that what is said should be criticized in the light of common sense. One of the reasons for the usefulness of such books as the monographs of Crowe and Cavalcaselle and of Symonds's *Michelangelo* is that they were intended for non-specialists. A non-specialized audience is also postulated in more recent books especially those that originate in lecturing. Fry's *Aspects of French Art*, his *Reflections on British Painting*, Sir Kenneth Clark's *Leonardo*, *The Nude*, and *Landscape into Art*, and Gombrich on *Art and Illusion* have it in common that they are thoroughly articulate. Lecturing has its dangers; not only can it lead, as it appeared to do with Fry, to over-simplified thought processes, but there is an entertainment factor built in to the lecture which is sometimes inimical to serious analysis. Its advantages however, are, very great; the text in lectures on the visual arts is almost always visual, the thought is generally clear-cut, and the style is that of spoken speech. When the skeleton of thought is filled out as fully as in the most accomplished of these volumes, Panofsky's *Early Netherlandish Painting*, the result is an ideally informative and ideally assimilable book.

The translation into English of the great German classics of art writing, Wölfflin's *Klassische Kunst* and *Kunstgeschichtliche Grundbegriffe*, Worringer's *Form in Gothic*, and the rest, has had less influence than might have been predicted forty years ago. The internationalizing of English art writing has been brought about by other means, largely by writers of German or Austrian origin, like Rudolf Wittkower and Niklaus Pevsner and Ernst Gombrich and Edgar Wind, who think in English and write with an exactness and flexibility that must excite the envy of those who have it as their native tongue. Here and there there is evidence of a seeming dissatisfaction with English as a means of art critical communication, which expresses itself in neologisms in an effort to invest with a wider meaning than they habitually carry terms that are actually in use. The word 'Quattrocento' is used to represent a style, not simply a period, the adjective 'classic' is distinguished from 'classical' and so on. Scarcely any of these usages have become general currency. In the field of art the finite character of English is an advantage not a handicap. Indeed one is tempted to believe that when some concept proves intractable in English, it is the concept not the language that is at fault.

As a branch of criticism writing on art is rather specially impermanent. What the art critic provides is an account of how works of art appear to the brain and retinal equipment of one individual at one point in time. Unless he can command the raft of eloquence on which Ruskin is still afloat, unless like Pater he can transmute art criticism into literature, or can make fundamental statements about the nature of artists or artefacts with the effortless simplicity of Berenson, he is expendable and in due course will be replaced. The factors that dictate his length of life are the closeness with which he engages with the work of art, and the clarity and honest-mindedness with which he sets down what he sees. At the end of the first act of Mozart's *Magic Flute* there is a famous scene in which Papageno asks Pamina what story they shall tell Sarastro, and Pamina replies, 'Die Wahrheit, die Wahrheit' [the truth, the truth]. Writing on art would be a more respected and indeed a more useful profession if it accepted the same goal of truthfulness.

# THE GIFF EDMONDS MEMORIAL LECTURE

This lecture is in memory of Nicholas Gifford Edmonds, of the 2nd Black Watch, who was killed at Magersfontein on 11 December 1899. It was founded by his sister, Miss Sophia Edmonds, a Member of this Society from 1919 to 1945.

---

# ON CONCEPTIONS OF GOOD GRAMMAR

*By* RANDOLPH QUIRK, M.A., PH.D., D.LIT.

*(Read 15 June 1967)*

*Baroness Stocks, B.Sc., LL.D., Litt.D., F.R.S.L., in the Chair*

MY title is not merely unattractive: it is misleading. I am not going to talk so much about instances of good or bad grammar as about the various meanings of the word 'grammar' itself. Even so, I shall not be taking all the various meanings of 'grammar' into account. I shall be limiting the discussion to a set which have, I think, particular relevance for us as writers, scholars, and teachers of English. I shall invite you to consider seven such meanings, choosing the number seven not so much with the Seven Sages of Greece in mind, still less the Seven Wonders of the World, or the Seven Names of God; not even with the Seven Deadly Sins in mind, or the Seven Years War, though these are more tempting associations. A better analogue is the part of London known as the Seven Dials. The name was given to a point from which seven streets radiated (as they still do) and at which there was a sun-dial which had faces visible from all these directions.

The image is not unfitting for a word like 'grammar' whose meanings go out in sharply different directions, and it has the added advantage of giving me an excuse to borrow the story which underlies the title of Martin Joos's book, *The Five Clocks* (The Hague, 1962, p. 7). Ballyhough railway station in Ireland has two clocks which disagree by some six minutes. When an irate traveller asked a porter what was the use of having two clocks if they didn't tell the same time, the porter replied, 'And what would we be wanting with two clocks if they told the same time?' I shall be claiming that we need the seven dials for grammar because they do not all tell the same time.

My starting-point is not, however, Ballyhough station but a leading article in the *Daily Telegraph* ten years ago which sparked off one of those recurrent high-temperature discussions that we have from time to time about the state of literacy among the younger generation. The leading article attributed the alleged decline in English usage to certain trends in modern educational theory and practice:

as the attention given to 'modern subjects' has increased, the liberal arts have had to be proportionately squeezed. Perhaps there is little point in sighing for the days when all the arts were indeed liberal: but the needs of a technocratic age are no excuse for neglect of the plain, simple machinery of our mother tongue. . . . The art of grammar was, after all, the traditional preoccupation of the grammar schools. Let them look to it. (31 August 1957.)

We shall not pause to wonder with what justification the writer thinks the machinery of our mother tongue is 'plain' and 'simple' or what he understands by 'liberal' when he wishes that the arts were still 'indeed liberal'. We must, however, take note that his weighty peroration uses 'grammar' in two distinct meanings in a single short sentence, the first being one that we shall explore here; the other (which is 'classical studies, especially Latin') being one we must otherwise ignore. Nor, I think, am I being unfair in picking on a technicality in the non-technical public press. Last year, the Incorporated Association of Assistant Masters issued the third edition of *The Teaching of English*, a work addressed to teachers in secondary schools, and we find a similar rhetorical use of the connection: 'All the boys and girls who come to grammar schools need some grammar' (Cambridge, 1966, p. 16).

But let us now look at the seven meanings which I should like to isolate for the purposes of our discussion today. I hope that each may be adequately both distinguished and illustrated in a single key sentence, and I also hope that the illustrations will show that all of these meanings are current, common, and non-technical.

1. *Latin has a good deal of grammar, but English has hardly any.*

The first of these meanings is in many respects also the narrowest. It is the one that has given rise to the common collocation 'grammar and syntax', thus carrying the implication that syntax is not a part of grammar. Its implications, however, go far beyond this. Clearly, it is a meaning that has emerged from the traditional identification, already mentioned, of grammar with classical and especially Latin studies. If grammar once meant the learning of Latin, it is natural that it should also come to mean inflexions or accidence, since inflexions play such a dominant role in Latin and preoccupy the learner's attention for a large part of his studies. Since one effect of the post-Renaissance cult of the vernaculars was to see them as fashioned in Latin's image, it was equally natural that linguistic study of them should focus on features analogous to the dominant ones in Latin. And since there were fewer inflexions in English, there was less 'grammar' and the notion of English as an easy language, a simplified language, grew up. Nor, I must insist, is this a trivial matter of popular parlance but an idea of long-standing among our leading thinkers. Thus, Sir Philip Sidney, towards the end of his essay *The Apologie for Poetrie*, accepts the criticism that English has little grammar but claims that this is a point in its favour, 'beeing so easie of it selfe, and so voyd of those cumbersome differences of Cases, Genders, Moodes, and Tenses, which I thinke was a peece of the Tower of *Babilons* curse'. Again, in his *Lectures on the English Language*, published a century ago, we find George Marsh referring to English as 'having no grammar', and so powerful did this belief become that few ever challenged the claims for the simplicity of Basic English that Ogden and Richards made on precisely these grounds.[1]

The second meaning that we should distinguish seems very similar to the first and indeed there are important connections:

2. *French has a good logical grammar but English is full of irregularities and idioms.*

Here again we are concerned with an informal comparison of two languages and here again English is regarded as being somehow deficient. But this time a good deal more than inflexions seems to be at issue, and you may agree that the mention of 'logic' in the first half of the illustrative sentence, and of 'idiom' in the second, shifts the emphasis rather to syntax. In other words, if 'grammar' in the first of our meanings excludes syntax, this second meaning tends if anything to exclude the inflexions with which the first meaning was virtually identified.

[1] See, however, Ifor Evans, *The Use of English* (2nd ed., London, 1966), especially pp. 54 ff.

Our second example raises, however, more important issues than this shift of emphasis. I think it is important to realize that whereas, given a Latin-orientated cultural history, the first meaning would seem true and obvious to the speaker of any language at all, this second meaning will seem most true and obvious to a native speaker of English. This is not a matter of the Anglo-Saxon sport of criticizing one's own institutions. It is a result of the fact that the native speaker learns the rules of his own language by a process which, although we know almost nothing about it, is quite different from and much less conscious than his way of learning a foreign language. This has the paradoxical effect that, while the native language remains the only language that most of us can use effortlessly, it is the *foreign* language whose rules we—in some sense—'know' and can repeat or explain. And since we find ourselves so often unable to explain to a foreigner or our own children the rules for a given construction, it readily seems to us that this is because—unlike the foreign language we have been laboriously taught—English has little regularity but much idiom. Testing this assertion is somewhat complicated by the educational and cultural background of an informant (notably in connection with the third meaning which we shall come to presently), but it is nevertheless quite easy to demonstrate the matter by asking a German tourist who is not a teacher of German to explain the rule about verbs with separable prefixes. He is quite likely to have greater difficulty doing so than an English boy preparing for 'O' Level German, and he is quite likely to end up with an apologetic smile saying that it is just idiomatic. Even, indeed, the points at which a native speaker feels there is complete regularity, he may find himself unable to state the rules and may therefore feel that there are none or only trivial, irrelevant, and self-evident ones. It is this situation which makes it difficult for the native English student to use even so excellent a book as the *Handbook of English Grammar* of R. W. Zandvoort (London, 1957), in the very first paragraph of which the third person singular present of English regular verbs is explained as follows:

[iz] is used after stems ending in a sibilant, [z] in other cases, except after breathed consonants, [s] after breathed consonants, except sibilants.

This accounts admirably for the difference between *he passes, he calls, he waits*, but is relevant only for the foreign learner; no native speaker, however young, is aware of any difference to be accounted for and that which needs no rules cannot easily be felt to have any.

We may now cautiously approach the third of our meanings, the illustrative sentence for which is as follows:

3. *French has a good, well-defined grammar but in English you're free to speak as you like.*

It will at once be clear why we need to be cautious at this point; the third meaning can easily be confused with the second that we have already considered, for the very good reason that English speakers usually make statements involving meaning two about those languages, such as French or Spanish or Italian, for which meaning three is also applicable. With meaning three, that is, we are concerned with the notion of an officially institutionalized grammar by a national academy. What the Swedes call *språkvård* and the Germans *Sprachpflege* may have small actual effect on linguistic usage, and the effect certainly varies from country to country, but one important effect is seen in the educational system. Where a language academy exists, there is usually a strong tradition for an insistent teaching of the rules so that young Frenchmen at least usually have a fair knowledge of the rules they break. Since this is so, it tends to perpetuate the false belief that we considered when we looked at the second meaning, namely, that every language has firm rules except English. It is significant that the Swedish and German words that I have just used cannot easily be translated into English; it is significant that the Society for Pure English remained a small and rather esoteric group without official backing and that it passed quietly out of existence some twenty years ago. We probably could not sustain a regular feature on such matters in the public press analogous to Robert le Bidois's *La Défense de la langue française* in *Le Monde*, and it would sound either facetious or jingoistic if it were called 'The Defence of English.' In the years around 1700, of course, the idea would have seemed more natural; in the context of the formation of the continental academies, numerous moves in this direction were made in England. If Swift had had his way, we might well have had a word today for *Sprachpflege*, and the word might have been 'ascertainment'. It will be recalled that Swift's famous *Proposal* of 1712 listed among the imperfections of English 'that in many instances it offends against every part of grammar'.[1]

[1] For a meticulous analysis of this use of 'grammar', see I. A. Richards, *Interpretation in Teaching* (London, 1938), pp. 212 ff.

The proposal was never adopted and to this day we lack the appeal to authority which is our third meaning of 'grammar'. While there is a strong popular tradition (its justification need not concern us) for appealing to '*the* dictionary' to prove whether or not a disputed word warrants the triumphant rejection, 'There's no such word', we cannot make a comparable appeal to '*the* grammar'. Some individual grammarians have come close to remedying the deficiency—Fowler in our own time, Latham a century ago, and, above all, Lindley Murray at the close of the eighteenth century. Indeed, the latter's *English Grammar* of 1795 defines his work in terms which clearly identify his concept of grammar with the meaning under discussion: 'the art of speaking and writing the English language with propriety.'

But with individual grammarians, we have in fact arrived at our fourth meaning:

4. *Jespersen wrote a good grammar but Nesfield's is boring.*

When we ask questions like 'Have you a Bible?' or 'Have you a Shakespeare?', we mean 'Have you a copy of the unchanging body of writing that we call "the Bible"?' ($\sim$ 'that comprises the work of Shakespeare?'). As I indicated above, there is a similar feeling for a body of unchanging data called 'the dictionary', and I suspect that when people say 'Have you a dictionary?' they often mean analogously 'Have you a copy of "the" dictionary?' We need have no such suspicions about the indefinite article with 'grammar', and as our example of the fourth meaning indicates, we are all thoroughly used to subjecting grammars to the sceptical appraisal that we adopt also for cookery books. Nor is the connection between grammars and cookbooks entirely inappropriate: the authors of both types of work are felt alike to begin with a mass of unstructured raw data and at their will they produce recipes for various occasions which we may like or dislike according to taste.

Thus, although meanings three and four resemble each other in referring to a codification of the rules for a particular language, they differ sharply in the degree of authority implied. And there are other differences which likewise spring from the individuality of the codification referred to with meaning four. Some grammars are written for mature scholars, some are written for schoolchildren; some are written for foreign learners, some for native speakers; some have the aim of giving the history of every construction, some are concerned only with the contemporary language. All these purposes result in sharply different organizations of what might be called 'the same' material. But there are still further ramifications to what 'grammar' in this fourth sense may mean. Where a 200-page grammar of modern French may be expected to deal almost exclusively with syntax and a 200-page grammar of Latin divide its attention between inflexions and syntax, a grammar of Old English or Old High German may with equal confidence be expected to present matter of an entirely different kind. In these latter cases, more than half the space is likely to be devoted to historical phonology, tracing the evolution of the vowels and consonants from Proto-Germanic or even Indo-European, with the bulk of the remainder devoted to a *non*-historical presentation of the inflexions; there may be nothing on the syntactical end of the grammatical spectrum at all.

The grammars in this fourth sense will also vary according to the grammatical theory embraced by their authors, and this brings us to the next meaning that we have to consider:

5. *Chomsky has devised a good grammar, but traditional grammar is unenlightening.*

This is the most abstract, elusive, and (in C. S. Lewis's[1] sense) 'dangerous' meaning that we have to consider. Since we are here concerned with the fundamental theories informing approaches to the study of language, the understanding of discussions involving this use of the word 'grammar' not merely requires that we understand the nature of the relation between a theory and the material it seeks to explicate: it requires also a fair degree of acquaintance with the specific theories. It goes without saying that the second of these conditions is quite often unfulfilled and so it would seem, all too frequently, is the first.

The complexity of the problem may be clearer if we consider an example. Let us suppose that we are trying to compare an observation on 'grammar' in sense five in the work of the late Professor W. J. Entwistle of Oxford with an observation on 'grammar', also in sense five, in the work of Professor R. B. Lees of Illinois. The effort to relate the two observations requires us to know and, if possible, to take account of the sharply different theories informing the two observations. To Entwistle, grammar is 'the construction placed by mind on the unorganized materials of speech. . . . That grammar is arbitrary

[1] Cf. *Studies in Words* (Cambridge, 1960), pp. 12 ff.

seems to become evident as we consider opposite ways of effecting the same end. No one device can be deemed more natural than another' (*Aspects of Language*, London, 1953, p. 145). To Lees, grammar is seen as 'a theory which will generate all and only grammatical sentences by means of naturally chosen, maximally simple, unrepeated rules' (*Language*, 33, 1957, p. 389). The one is imposing an arbitrary, consciously unnatural order on chaos; the other is simulating the natural creative potentiality in the human linguistic mechanism. It may well be as difficult to relate statements by these two scholars as it is to relate the work of a geologist to that of an architect. Yet this is the problem that confronts us—all the more frightening for being unacknowledged—when we find teachers eager to reject 'traditional grammar' and to replace it by 'the new grammar'. On the one hand, there is being rejected an approach whose 2,000-year-old theoretical basis is quite possibly not understood: in other words, even if one agreed with the rejection one cannot easily be sure one is agreeing with the motives for rejection. On the other hand, there is not one new grammar but many (some of them very old but writ new) and they have many different aims. In other words, it may be right to discontinue geology and to study architecture in its place but we must not propose such a change under the impression that architecture is merely an improved form of geology.

It is with some relief that we turn to the sixth meaning of 'grammar' which is decidedly easier to understand:

6. *John uses good grammar, but his spelling is awful.*

In juxtaposing the most difficult and theoretical meaning with the easiest and most practical (as well as probably the most common), I am of course leading up to a full realization of the confusion that conceptions of 'good grammar' can produce. But for the present let us notice two aspects of this sixth sense. In the first place, it seems worth noting that in the most ordinary and non-technical discourse people clearly conceive of 'good grammar' as having a relatively well-defined reference within the totality of linguistic usage such that it certainly excludes spelling and pronunciation and probably with equal definiteness excludes use of vocabulary items and the meaning of words as well. If a child is found using *interloper* where he should be using *interpreter*, no one is likely to say that this is bad grammar. In the second place, let us consider whether even this sixth meaning of grammar is as easy to understand as we thought.

If we carefully exclude from our minds the earlier senses (particularly the fourth), then we may agree that

  6a. *John has a good knowledge of grammar*

refers to sentence structure, sequence of tenses, case, number, and the like, whether it is expanded as

  6b. *John has a good knowledge of grammar and his sentences are very shapely*

or as

  6c. *John has a good knowledge of grammar but he can't write correct English.*

It may well be objected that the apparent incompatibility is occasioned by the ambiguity of 'knowledge' rather than the ambiguity of 'grammar', and I would be prepared to agree. But the fact remains that, to the extent that (6b) and (6c) are sensible, meaningful sentences, they show that it is possible to conceive of a knowledge of grammar which informs or preconditions our use of a language, and a knowledge of the same grammatical data that exists independently of our ability to use the language. We may notice in this connection that it would make sense to say of an English child

  6d. *He knows no grammar but he speaks correct English*

but not to say

  6e. *He knows no grammar but he speaks correct French.*

This is tantamount to admitting that the grammatical data we are discussing when we use 'grammar' in the sixth meaning are part of a natural ability in relation to the native language, and that, unlike the grammatical data of a foreign language, the teachers's task is only to make the learner aware of what he knows already.

In speaking of the teacher's task, we have arrived at 'grammar' as a curricular subject, our seventh and final sense:

  7. *English grammar is good but I hate arithmetic.*

In introducing the sixth meaning, I said it was probably the commonest and least technical, and if I am right in feeling that this seventh meaning is almost as common and as commonplace, we might well expect a good deal of direct correspondence between them—especially as both so obviously share the aura of the schoolroom. But in fact we find here a source of fresh confusion. It will be recalled that the sixth meaning clearly excluded spelling, pronunciation, vocabulary, and so on. Curiously perhaps (and certainly unfortunately), there are no similar limits on 'grammar' as a subject. Let me quote again from the 1966 edition of the I.A.A.M. handbook on *The Teaching of English*:

> The aim of a grammar lesson . . . is to create an interest in words . . . Investigation into their origin and meaning is nearly always popular and useful. Here the appeal is mainly historical. More exciting is the attack on neologisms, which takes us straight into such splendid fields as American English, slang, modern science . . . Latin and Greek roots . . . English spelling . . . the traditional rules for pronunciation . . . (pp. 15–16).

However 'exciting' and 'splendid' these activities may be, they are very much wider and more varied than meaning six would lead us to expect: the 'good grammar' that John is taught by no means corresponds to the 'good grammar' that John is judged to know or use. So it is that, within the same classroom, it makes sense to utter both sentence (6) and also

7*a*. *Grammar is good when it consists of spelling-bees.*

Splendid and exciting it undoubtedly is, but let it be perfectly clear to us all that it is not 'grammar' in any of the six earlier senses that we have examined.

Let us now turn back to our starting-point, the *Daily Telegraph* leading article. What is it that this article is seeking to reinstate in schools? Is it the same as what Mr. David Holbrook has recently referred to as 'the old grammar grind?'[1] And if it is, why should anyone want to reintroduce something of which Holbrook so resoundingly disapproves? It surely cannot be that Holbrook would call an 'old grind' what the Incorporated Association of Assistant Masters calls 'splendid' and 'exciting'. We have seen of course that there are several points at which confusion can arise through the sharply different meanings possessed by the word 'grammar' and that there are other points (for example, meaning one itself) at which prejudice can grow up against the idea of teaching English grammar. What greater waste of time is conceivable?

Confusion is worse confounded, however, when we look at some of the ways in which 'the art of grammar' is actually handled in schools. The Educational Institute of Scotland in 1939 issued a statement on *The Junior Secondary School*, in which it was claimed that 'The function of grammar [our meaning

---

[1] *The Exploring Word* (Cambridge, 1967), p. 182.

seven, of course] is to assist pupils to read with understanding and to speak and write correctly' [i.e. to acquire
good grammar in meaning six]; it is, in short, 'a practical aid
to composition'. We should note that it is an untested assumption
that 'grammar' in meaning seven can lead to the acquisition of
'grammar' in meaning six, and we need not be surprised that
it remains an assumption when we hear how grammar 'seven' is
taught in the very schools that come within the Institute's
purview. W. J. Macauley has told us[1] of a 'typical scheme of
work to be covered in the primary school' as 'used in Glasgow'.
Daily classes of about half an hour are as follows: at the age of
7½ years, pupils have lessons on the noun and the verb, singular
and plural number; at 8 the study of adjectives is added; at 8½
personal pronouns and the tenses of verbs. How children have
managed with verbs but no tenses for a whole year is unex-
plained. Despite this, says Macauley, teachers complain that
'pupils entering the secondary school appear to show a complete
lack of understanding of even the terms of grammar'. That is,
not only is composition presumably unaided but pupils have not
even acquired the patter implied in sentence (6c). And in case
this example suggests that the situation is especially deplorable
in Scotland, let me just quote from the English Association's
publication of 1946, *The Teaching of English in Schools*, in which
it is stated that 'the more formal parts of grammar could, in
view of their simplicity in English, be mastered between the ages
of 10 and 12'. If 'grammar' is being used in senses one or two,
then we have seen that it is not 'simple' for English but that it
would, of course, have indeed been mastered by the age of 10;
so there is nothing to teach in any case. If it is being used in
sense seven (the only other possibility), then we have seen from
the Scottish experiences that it is unlikely to be learnt by the
age of 12 and that its usefulness would be highly questionable
even if it were.

It is not part of my purpose today to say in what sense—if any
—grammar should be 'looked to' in grammar schools, but it
occurs to me that grammar-school pupils could do worse than
be taught to understand the many ways in which the word
'grammar' is used in discourse about language. In particular,
since every normal person seems to have a keen interest in
speculating about the nature of his own language, it might
be of special interest to help people to understand meanings
two, four, and five, and the relation between them. Thus it is

[1] *British Journal of Educational Psychology*, 17 (1947).

interesting (and apparently not obvious) that every language is an elaborate code of rules, and every one to a greater or lesser extent a different code. This is meaning two, and further consideration of it (by means, for example, of sentence 2) brings home to us the subjective apprehension that the codes are different in kind—notably that the code of one's native language is very differently apprehended from the code of a language that we learn as a foreign language. And this leads us to consider the presumably very different learning mechanisms that are involved, differing perhaps more in terms of the age at which we learn the native language than in terms of the method ('direct', 'translation', etc.) by which we learn a foreign language.

These different codes invite the construction of theories to account for language rules, the best way to describe them, the best way to regard their relationship to each other and to the rest of human behaviour. This is grammar in sense five. And finally, we come to applications of a grammar in sense five to a grammar in sense two in order to produce a grammar in sense four—a book which sets out the code of a particular language, setting it out, that is, in a form that is quite different from the code in its natural state (as the language itself) and made interestingly accessible for intellectual examination as distinct from practical use.

The convincingness of such a three-way relationship between senses two, four, and five may be increased by comparing a projected (and perhaps more readily recognizable) three-way relationship in the field of vocabulary. It probably requires little effort to realize that every language has its own vocabulary, seen as a large stock of separate names for things and qualities and activities, and that every language's word stock is to a greater or lesser degree independent of every other language's. This corresponds to grammar in sense two. Now as soon as we start cataloguing the wordstock, we realize we have to think of what exactly a word is, what we are going to call a word for our cataloguing purposes: is *goodbye* or *how do you do* a word because *cheerio* and *hello* seem to be? But then what about *good night*? How many words are there in *Thank you, il y a, gas stove, railway station refreshment room, Eintrittsgeld*? And there are other considerations: should my catalogue give the history of the words, their pronunciation, their meaning? Should it try to include everything like the latest big *Webster* or try to be selective like the latest *Concise Oxford*? These theoretical matters are clearly analogous to and perhaps valuable in explaining grammar in sense five. And then finally there are the catalogues themselves which make the vocabulary accessible, however oddly abstracted from the language and even more oddly ordered: the catalogues that we call dictionaries and which bring together the theory (as in 'grammar five') with the material of the specific language (as in 'grammar two') to form a description after the manner of 'grammar four'.

It is not claimed that any such organization of our conceptions of grammar or other aspects of linguistic form will help the *Daily Telegraph* to remedy the nation's bad grammar. But at least it may direct our attention (and that of our pupils) towards the nature of good grammar itself.

# KATJA REISSNER LECTURE

This lecture perpetuates the memory of Katja Reiss-
ner, musician, and lover of literature, who died in
December 1952. It was founded by her son, Alexander
Reissner, a Member of this Society since 1946.

---

# GEORGE IV: PATRON OF LITERATURE

### By JOANNA RICHARDSON, M.A., F.R.S.L.

*(Read 1 December 1966)*

*Robert Rhodes James, M.A., F.R.S.L., in the Chair*

PATRONAGE—like writing itself—is a natural gift and an art
that demands assiduous practice. The ideal patron of literature
is more than a rich philanthropist: indeed I would suggest that
wealth is not his most important asset. It is more necessary that
he should be a man of instinctive taste, a man of liberal mind
and cultivated intellect, a man of sense and sensibility. The
ideal patron should be a man with broad and lively interests, a
man of vision, a man who is concerned with humankind as
much as he is concerned with their achievements. The ideal
patron is, above all, personal; he is concerned with the
individual writer. For it is by encouraging individuals that
he fulfils his most important task: he provides the warm,
sympathetic atmosphere which is necessary for creative work.
Literature—like love—is unlikely to blossom in a cold climate.

Kings and queens are of course the greatest potential patrons
of their time. 'We are the makers of manners', said Shakespeare's
Henry V. Max Beerbohm only enlarged the phrase when he
wrote in his essay *King George the Fourth*: 'George was a splendid
patron. . . . Indeed, he inspired society with a love of something
more than mere pleasures, a love of the "humaner delights".
He was a giver of tone.'

We might remember George IV as a friend of music; we
might remember him—indeed, we cannot forget him—as a
lover of the visual arts, of painting, sculpture, architecture,
furniture, and fashion. It seems appropriate that this evening

we should remember him as our founder—as a patron of literature.

George Augustus Frederick, the 21st Prince of Wales, was born on 12 August 1762. He was the eldest child of George III and Charlotte of Mecklenberg-Strelitz. He spent the early years of his childhood at Kew Palace, and his first English teacher, a Miss Margaret Planta, was, we are told, 'quiet, patient, plodding, persevering'. When the Prince of Wales was 9, and his brother the Duke of York was 8, Dr. William Markham was appointed their preceptor. Dr. Markham combined the post with two others of importance: he was Dean of Christ Church, Oxford, and he was Bishop of Chester. However, for a short time each year he contrived to live at Kew, where he supervised the two eldest princes. At the age of 12, the Prince of Wales wrote: 'Your good instruction, your kindness, your good nature, will never be effaced from my heart.' No doubt he owed much of his taste for the classics to his 'dear and much-loved Friend'. Dr. Markham fostered the best traits of the Prince of Wales: his natural taste, and his natural warmth of heart.

However, in 1776, for a quite inadequate reason, George III dismissed Dr. Markham, and replaced him by Dr. Hurd, the Bishop of Lichfield and Coventry. Dr. Hurd drew up an exacting curriculum for the princes, which included religion and morals, history, government and laws, mathematics, natural philosophy, and polite literature. Dr. Hurd was a demanding tutor: 'Greek for some time omitted,' he noted, 'except on Sunday mornings, when the Greek testament is to be constantly read.' However, this disciplinarian treatment seems to have carried the Prince's gratitude: forty years later, as George IV, he still spoke about his preceptors with particular affection.

The Prince of Wales's education was in many ways deplorably inadequate. Whatever Dr. Hurd decreed, no one roused his interest in the art of government; no one really taught him the principles of politics or statesmanship, or gave him unforgettable moral instruction. He was left in ignorance of social conditions. Yet by the time he was 18, he must have been among the most accomplished princes in Europe.

His knowledge of the ancient languages was [we are told] correct and extensive, and he could converse with ease and fluency in French, German and Italian. The best English writers, particularly poets, were familiar to His Royal Highness; and on all the subjects relating to belles lettres there were few critics who possessed a purer taste or a more refined judgment.

In 1796, when William Ireland, the forger, claimed to have found a mass of Shakespeare's papers, the Prince summoned him to bring them to Carlton House. He showed a disconcerting knowledge of Elizabethan documents, and he questioned Ireland with an acuteness which Ireland 'had never before witnessed from the learned'. The Prince suspected the forgery which Ireland later confessed. One thing, he said, was perfectly clear: there were too many manuscripts to have been hidden above ground for so long.

There was, however, one cache of buried treasure which had caught the Prince's imagination: this was the ancient library at Herculaneum. It was in 1713 that some Neapolitan labourers, sinking a well, had unearthed a statue in the theatre of Herculaneum. One thousand six hundred and thirty-four years after the eruption of Vesuvius, under 24 feet of volcanic matter, the city of Herculaneum was refound. In 1752, 'most wonderfully preserved, under a stupendous mass of volcanick substance', archaeologists had uncovered a great number of blackened rolls, which were at first mistaken for lumps of charcoal. Many of the rolls were destroyed, before someone discovered that they were an ancient library of papyri. During the next half-century, eighteen of these papyri were opened and deciphered; and, judging by the date of the eruption, it seemed that scholars might recover works by the most famous writers in antiquity.

It needed a philanthropic prince with respect for literature, for ancient history and scholarship, to patronize the ambitious enterprise. In 1800, with the consent of the Neapolitan Government, the Prince of Wales undertook to have all the remaining papyri unrolled and copied at his own expense. He sent out the Revd. John Hayter, Fellow of King's College, Cambridge, to direct the work.

Hayter arrived in Palermo in 1800, and at last, in 1802, they began to unfold the papyri in the Royal Museum of Portici, near Naples. An Italian chemist was recommended for the task, and —as Hayter remembered—he was allowed to treat the papyri with 'vegetable gas'. The result was catastrophic. 'The greatest part of each mass flew, under this trial, into useless atoms. . . . The dreadful odour drove us all from the Museum.' The chemical disaster was followed by a political crisis. About 200 papyri had been opened, and nearly 100 of them had been copied, when, in 1806, came the French invasion. The

Neapolitan Court emigrated to Palermo, and Hayter was obliged to abandon the papyri, and to hurry off to Palermo with facsimiles.

For the next three years he supervised the making of engravings, and composed a Latin poem, 'Herculaneum', which he dedicated to the Prince of Wales. Sir William Drummond, who was sometime Minister to Naples, made it clear that Hayter also indulged in less academic activities.

> The stories of your battles in brothels, &c., [wrote Sir William] made so much noise, and were multiplied so fast, that I found it impossible to apologise for your conduct. In the midst of all the confusion which this conduct created, you suddenly left Palermo, without indicating where you were going. . . . I then determined to take the MSS. into my own hands.

In 1809 the errant scholar was ordered back to England; he brought home ninety-four facsimiles of papyri, and some engravings. The Herculaneum Mission had not fulfilled its patron's expectations; but—as a versifier proclaimed—the Prince of Wales had shown himself a practical and enlightened lover of scholarship.

> Th' illustrious HEIR of Britain's Royal Throne,
> Attach'd to science, makes its cause his own:
> Treasures long hid—to human eye deny'd,
> Since cities vanish'd, and since Pliny died!
> The letter'd wealth Vesuvius whelm'd in night
> His Princely bounty brings once more to light!
> Matchless in manners, and in taste refin'd,
> He knows that Genius is the wealth of mind;
> And still in Learning's noblest interests true,
> Becomes its PATRON, and its Votary too . . .

In 1810 the Prince of Wales presented the fruits of the Herculaneum Mission to Oxford, and the University gave him the degree of Doctor of Civil Law.

The Prince of Wales—who might well have read Greats—showed more than a taste for the classics; he had a keen historical sense. When Nelson died, it was the Prince who asked that his papers should be collected, and that a Life of Nelson should be written. The Prince's librarian helped to produce the eight-volume work.

The Prince of Wales, who had been Nelson's friend, also showed a lifelong and romantic devotion to the Stuarts. In 1804, Sir John Hippisley, his agent in Italy, had begun negotiations to retrieve the Stuart family papers. In 1805, before Nelson set out on his last voyage, Sir John had asked him to obtain the documents, which had been moved from Rome to Civita Vecchia, and deposited with a British merchant. Alas, a year later the merchant, a Mr. Bertram, was rumoured to be in prison, 'seized on and confined by the French'. The Prince of Wales refused to give up the search. In 1810 he told Sir John to authorize a certain Mr. Bonelli to obtain the Stuart documents. It was Bonelli, we are told,

who at length, though with considerable risk, . . . succeeded in shipping off the Cases for Leghorn, and having there concealed them from the vigilance of the Customs House Officers, they were with great difficulty embarked on a Tunisian vessel bound to Tunis, and thence forwarded to Malta and finally to London, when the whole were placed in the Library at Carlton House.

In 1816, Longman's finally published two solid volumes: *The Life of James II, King of England, Collected out of Materials Writ of his own Hand*. The preservation and publication of these documents was almost entirely due to the Prince's zeal.

Years later, when the Prince was king, his surgeon, Sir Astley Cooper, ventured rather rashly to mention the Stuarts.

I once said, 'Sire, are you familiar with the fate of Henrietta Maria, after the death of Charles I? It is to be found, I believe, in Pennant.' 'Oh,' he said, 'read De Grammont; there you will find all about her, together with the history of those times, well described, and minutely given.'

Dates, also, in history, he could well recollect, [added Sir Astley Cooper] and it was dangerous to differ with him concerning them, as he was sure to be right.

The Prince of Wales was a classical scholar, and something of an historian; he was also constantly concerned with modern literature. In 1804 the Royal Literary Fund—as it is called today—needed 'a Collegiate Retreat for a Few Literary Benefactors of Mankind'. The council were worried about the cost of a house; the Prince of Wales offered 200 guineas a year for his lifetime, and immediately stabilized the society.

But though literary patronage may be dispensed through an institution, it is most heart-warming, most effective when it comes from an individual, when it springs from a personal relationship; and the most endearing sign of the Prince's love of literature was his interest in living writers. He delighted in showing appreciation of men of artistic or intellectual distinction. It was not that he felt it part of his duty: it was that he admired and understood men of creative mind, and men of intellect. He enjoyed their friendship, and he rejoiced that he could cultivate it.

In 1800, a young and ambitious Irish poet and lyric-writer, Thomas Moore, received permission to dedicate his translation of Anacreon to the Prince of Wales. Soon afterwards, he was presented to the Prince himself.

He is beyond doubt a man of very fascinating manners [Moore wrote home to his mother]. . . . He said he was very happy to know a man of *my abilities*; and when I thanked him for the honour he did me in permitting the dedication of Anacreon, he stopped me and said, the honour was *entirely* his, in being allowed to put his name to a work of such merit. He then said that he hoped, when he returned to town in the winter, we should have many opportunities of *enjoying each other's society*; that he was passionately fond of music, and had long heard of my talents in that way. Is not all this very fine?

The Prince was a little Irish at heart, and he warmed to Moore; he introduced him to Mrs. Fitzherbert, and when he gave his grand entertainment at Carlton House, in the first months of the Regency, Moore was invited, and enchanted by the Regent's friendliness, and by the fantastic splendour, the theatrical invention of the décor.

My dearest Mother,

I ought to have written yesterday, but I was in bed all day after the fête, which I did not leave till past six in the morning. Nothing was ever half so magnificent. . . . The Prince spoke to me, as he always does, with the cordial familiarity of an old acquaintance.

In an age of rigid class distinction, when every Exclusive shrank from contact with a Nobody, the Prince was an ideal patron of the arts; he showed not only his natural taste, and his practical interest, but he was charmingly accessible.

The friendship which he showed to Moore was enough to gratify any human being—let alone an ambitious poet. It seems extraordinary that Moore should have thrown it away for the sake of party politics. But this was precisely what he did.

For many years he had set his hopes of a comfortable sinecure on his friendship with the Regent's friend, Lord Moira. In March 1812, Moira fell from favour, and a few months later the Regent chose a Tory government. Moore's prospects of advancement seemed to be dashed. There was no more point in playing safe, and in 1813 he published *Intercepted Letters, or the Twopenny Postbag*. This sharp little book of political squibs was tossed off with more Irish wit than prudence: indeed, Moore showed himself to be reckless to the point of lunacy. His gibes

at the corpulent Regent and his Egeria, the middle-aged Lady
Hertford, in Manchester Square, put him, once and for all,
beyond the pale.

> Through Manchester Square took a canter just now—
> Met the *old yellow chariot*, and made a low bow.
> This I did, of course, thinking 'twas loyal and civil,
> But got such a look—oh 'twas black as the devil!
> How unlucky!—*incog.* he was travelling about,
> And I, like a noodle, must go find him out!
>
> *Mem.*—When next by the old yellow chariot I ride,
> To remember there *is* nothing Princely inside.

Moore turned against the Regent for political reasons—and,
one feels, out of sheer perversity. Many people turned against
the Regent because of his unhappy domestic life. English writers
were not always models of domestic fidelity or felicity—but
somehow they could not forgive the Regent for his treatment of
his unbalanced wife, or for the consolation he found with other
women. Shelley believed in free love, as we know, and he was
no doubt a cause of his first wife's suicide; yet he still described
the Regent as 'that infernal wretch', and he dismissed Carlton
House as an Augean stable, thick 'with filth which no second
Hercules could cleanse'. Leigh Hunt was imprisoned for a
savage personal libel on the Regent, or, as he put it, 'for not
thinking the Prince Regent slender and laudable'. Keats wrote
to his sister: 'I can pass a summer very quietly without caring
about Fat Louis, [Louis XVIII] fat Regent or the Duke of
Wellington.' Charles Lamb, at the time of the Coronation,
cried: 'Long live the Queen! Death to the King!' 'Vivat
Regina! Moriatur ***!' And Byron came in time to write
harsh verses on George IV's state visit to Ireland. It is Byron's
antagonism to George IV which is most to be regretted, for—
like Tom Moore's—it was largely perversity.

In 1812, when *Childe Harold's Pilgrimage* made Byron the
demigod of Society, the Regent asked that he should be presented. Byron was conquered—as Moore had been—and in time
he paid grudging tribute in *Don Juan*:

> There, too, he saw (whate'er he may be now)
>     A Prince, the Prince of Princes at the time.
> With fascination in his very bow,
>     And full of promise, as the spring of prime.
> Though Royalty was written on his brow,
>     He had *then* the grace, too, rare in every clime,

Of being, without alloy of fop or beau,
A finished Gentleman from top to toe.

Byron's conversation with the Regent in 1812 inspired more than a stanza in *Don Juan*. It had been very largely about Walter Scott, and since the attack on Scott in *English Bards and Scotch Reviewers*, there had naturally been a breach between Scott and the 'young whelp of a Lord Byron'. Both Byron and John Murray, his publisher, saw the Regent's comments as a means of healing the breach, and Byron duly sent Scott an account of the conversation:

And now . . . let me talk to you of the Prince Regent. He ordered me to be presented to him at a ball; and after some sayings peculiarly pleasing from royal lips, as to my own attempts, he talked to me of you and your immortalities: he preferred you to every bard past and present. . . . He spoke alternately of Homer and yourself, and seemed well acquainted with both, so that you were in very good company. I defy Murray to have exaggerated his Royal Highness's opinion of your powers, nor can I pretend to enumerate all he said on the subject; but it may give you pleasure to hear that it was conveyed in language which would only suffer by my attempting to transcribe it, and with a tone and taste which gave me a very high idea of his abilities and accomplishments, which I had hitherto considered as confined to *manners*, certainly superior to those of any living *gentleman*. . . .

Scott replied, from Abbotsford, with becoming modesty:

I am much indebted to your Lordship for your kind and friendly letter; and much gratified by the Prince Regent's good opinion of my literary attempts. . . . It is a fortunate thing for the Prince himself that he has a literary turn, since nothing can so effectually relieve the ennui of state, and the anxieties of power.

The Regent's 'literary turn' had not only healed the breach between Scott and Byron; it had established a friendship between them. Byron himself was delighted by his glimpse of royal favour: in fact, he wrote gaily to Lord Holland that he might one day be Poet Laureate. He was not as flippant as he tried to suggest: soon afterwards, a visitor found him in court dress, with his fine black hair in powder, preparing to attend the Regent's levée.

It is tempting to speculate how different Byron's life and poetry might have been if he had become Poet Laureate: if he had tried to fit the conventional world. However, the levée was postponed; and, as far as we know, Byron never spoke to the Regent again. He found it hard to imagine himself writing odes at Court. 'My politics being as perverse as my rhymes, I had, in fact,' he said, 'no business there.'

He had indeed no business there. In 1812 the *Morning Chronicle* had published two discreetly anonymous stanzas to the Regent's daughter, Princess Charlotte. In 1814, thanks to Byron's political perversity, the stanzas were republished over his name.

## TO A LADY WEEPING

Weep, daughter of a royal line,
  A sire's disgrace, a realm's decay;
Ah, happy! if each tear of thine
  Could wash a father's fault away!

Weep—for thy tears are virtue's tears—
  Auspicious to these suffering isles;
And be each drop in future years
  Repaid thee by thy people's smiles.

The publication naturally created an uproar. The Press, said Byron, went into hysterics, and his publisher was in a fright. The Regent himself had attributed the lines to Moore; he was sad rather than angry when he learned that Byron had written them. No doubt he regretted that such comments should come from a poet whom he had recently thought a friend.

In 1813—the year when Moore had published *The Twopenny Postbag*—two literary events had claimed the Regent's attention. The first was the arrival of Mme de Staël. The turbulent author of *De la Littérature*, Mme de Staël had dared to compare the age in which she lived with the decadent pre-Christian Roman Empire. She had thus incurred the displeasure of Napoleon. The only continental Power who had resisted him as steadfastly as England, she had now been exiled for the third time from France. In the summer of 1813, she descended on London with her daughter, her elder son, and Rocca, her handsome young lover, to excite the envy of her own sex and enjoy the honours due to her talents. Soon after her arrival, John Murray bought the manuscript of *De l'Allemagne* for 1,500 guineas. The book was published in October, and sold out in three days.

Mme de Staël was the most invited person in the metropolis, the literary lioness of the season; she was sought by all society, and not least by the Regent, who wanted to invite her to his fête. Since etiquette demanded that she should have been presented first, the Regent went to a soirée himself, to meet her. Mme de Staël was large, coarse, and homely, with a total want of grace and beauty, but he appreciated women of intellect. He sat beside her, so she said, for three-quarters of an hour, and was 'on ne peut pas être plus aimable'. Henceforward Mme de Staël was constantly singing the Regent's praises, and the Regent was always singing hers. Since he had a true sense of distinction, he himself called on her at the house she had taken in George Street. She stayed in England for nearly a year —until the fall of Napoleon.

The other literary event in the summer of 1813 was the death of Mr. Pye, the Poet Laureate, and the search for someone to succeed him. The world of intriguers and poets was astir. The Revd. James Stanier Clarke, the Regent's librarian, who was never lacking in assurance, decided to support a candidate. He had sent presentation copies of his own books to Scott, and Scott had acknowledged them in flattering terms; and though Clarke had never actually met the author of *Marmion*, he now liked to consider him a friend. On 18 August, full of his own minuscule importance, Clarke 'delivered' to the Regent his 'warmest wish and anxious desire' that Scott should have the post. The Regent, so Clarke wrote to Scott, 'replied "that you had already been written to, and that if you wished it everything would be settled as I could desire".' Mr. Clarke then offered Scott his congratulations.

Unfortunately, they were premature. When Scott received the formal offer of the Laureateship from the Marquis of Hertford, he did not accept it by return of post. As a family man, he was tempted by the thought of the salary; as a self-respecting poet, he felt inclined to refuse the official status. Early in September he sent an unctuous refusal to Lord Hertford, and a courtly letter to Stanier Clarke. He contrived to keep his independence and, as he expressed it, 'every sentiment of loyalty'.

He had also borne another candidate in mind: a candidate who had for years been angling for a sinecure. This was the poet and historian Robert Southey. 'I have declined the appointment,' wrote Scott. 'Will you forgive me, my dear friend, if I own I had you in my recollection?' Southey—who was eating oysters at Streatham—wrote at once to his warm supporter, Mr. Croker, the Secretary to the Admiralty. He could not, he said, write poems to order, like a schoolboy; but 'if it were understood that upon great public events I might either write or be silent as the spirit moved, I should now accept the office as an honourable distinction'. Mr. Croker replied, very justly, 'that it was not for us to make terms with the Prince Regent. "Go you," said he, "and write your Ode for the New Year. You can never have a better subject than the present state of the war affords you."'

Southey found a better subject. A few weeks afterwards, the muse descended; and he addressed some lines to his wife:

> I have something to tell you, which you will not be sorry at,
> 'Tis that I am sworn in to the office of Laureat . . .
> Keep this, I pray you, as a precious gem,
> For this is the Laureat's first poem.

No doubt Mrs. Southey forgave her husband the style for the sake of the content.

As for Walter Scott, who had refused the poetic laurel, he managed dexterously to keep in royal favour. He had for years been a friend of the wretched Princess of Wales. In 1811, when the Prince of Wales became Regent, Scott had expressed grave doubts of his prudence, and he had become rigidly puritan. And then came Byron's flattering conversation with the Regent; and hints reached Scott that the Regent would like to see him. His loyalties became more complicated.

In 1815, when the Princess of Wales had gone abroad, Scott found it easier to obey the Regent's wishes. Once he had eagerly sent *Marmion* to the Princess; now he sent *The Lord of the Isles* to her husband. Mr. Stanier Clarke replied 'that the Prince Regent particularly wishes to see you whenever you come to London; and desires you will always, when you are there, come into his library whenever you please'. When Croker announced that Scott would be in town by the middle of March, the Regent answered: 'Let me know when he comes, and I'll get up a snug little dinner that will suit him.' Scott was presented at the levée: 'a tall, very simple, but benevolent looking man of middle age, who spoke broad Scotch.' He was invited to dinner, and delighted the Prince Regent with his anecdotes of the old Scottish judges. The Regent capped some of his stories, and doubtless gave one or two of the famous imitations which would make even Wellington helpless with laughter. And perhaps it was on this occasion that they eagerly discussed their mutual hero, the Young Pretender. The only difference between them was that the Regent spoke of 'the Pretender', and Scott spoke rigorously of 'Prince Charles'.

On all his later visits to London, Scott was a frequent guest at the royal table. After his first royal interview, he himself decided that the Regent was 'the first gentleman he had seen—certainly the first *English* gentleman of his day;—there was something about him which, independently of the *prestige*, the "divinity," which hedges a King, marked him as standing entirely by himself'. Before Scott returned to the north, the Regent sent him a gold snuffbox, set with brilliants. It was his tangible tribute to 'genius & merit'.

Scott was determined to exploit such favour. The following year he begged Croker to ask if he might search for the Scottish regalia.

On the union of England and Scotland in 1707, the Scottish crown and sceptre and sword of state had been deposited in a strong box in the Crown Room of Edinburgh Castle. It had been decreed that they should never be taken out of Scotland. Rumour said that they had since been spirited away. On Scott's insistence, Croker now asked the Regent to authorize a search. The mystery, with its Stuart connections, caught the Regent's imagination, and early in 1818 Croker announced that the royal consent had been given. Scott might have been expected to show his gratitude for the Regent's understanding; but sometimes, as one contrasts his public conduct, his courtly manners, with his private comments, one feels that affection and self-interest, civility and vulgarity went hand in hand. Now, in a private letter, he revealed his coarse hypocrisy: 'Our fat friend has remembered a petition which I put up to him. . . . Our fat friends curiosity goes to the point at once.'

On 4 February 1818, Scott and his fellow Commissioners proceeded, with due pomp, to Edinburgh Castle. They solemnly opened the sealed doors to the Crown Room, and broke open the strong box which had been locked for over a century. That hazy winter afternoon, at about 4 o'clock, the sound of cannon from the Castle announced that the crown of the old kings was discovered.

It was the moment to cement the friendship with the Regent. A draughtsman was asked to make sketches of the regalia 'which His Royal Highness's goodness has restored to light and honour'. The Regent was at least sent a likeness of the crown which, as Scott privately informed a correspondent, had never been 'profaned by the touch of a monarch of a foreign dynasty'.

It was towards the end of the year, and, apparently, on his own initiative, that the Regent decided to make Scott a baronet. The author of *Ivanhoe* had long seen himself in a feudal setting, and he had designed the mock-Gothic splendours of Abbotsford

ical methods is expectations,d better if Davy had not
sent out an Oxford scholar, Peter Elmsley, later, to decipher
the inscriptions. The Neapolitans were enraged. 'They are not
so jealous of Sir Humphry as of me,' wrote Elmsley. 'They say
that they have eight critical scholars in constant pay and
employment, and the deuce is in it if they want the assistance
of a ninth from Oxford. I suspect that the affair will end in
smoke.'

And so it did. The arrival of Elmsley finally wrecked the
Herculaneum Mission. The Neapolitan scholars became so
jealous, and so obstructionist, that it seemed a waste of public
money and a compromise of character to continue. The enthusiasm
and imagination, the taste and generosity of George IV had
been poorly rewarded.

The Herculaneum Mission was finally abandoned soon after
George IV came to the throne. And, almost at the same time,
the King embarked on his most enduring literary venture.

The original idea came from Dr. Thomas Burgess, who was
then the Bishop of St. David's. In October 1820 Dr. Burgess was

considering the state of the nation; and he did so with a certain satisfaction. The Napoleonic Wars were over, Napoleon was exiled on St. Helena, and Great Britain had reached a peak of moral influence and military glory. Every European nation admired her character and her institutions. 'Amongst all these noble and useful Institutions,' wrote the Bishop, 'must it not strike them with astonishment, that there has never existed in the British Metropolis, a Society for the Encouragement and Improvement of General Learning and Polite Literature?' It seemed essential to civilized life and to national prestige that there should be some sort of English equivalent to the Académie-Française.

On 2 November the Bishop had an audience of the King to discuss 'this infant undertaking'. King George IV—so he remembered—showed 'the warmth and interest of the most devoted friend to Literature'. He promised him his patronage and his financial support. That afternoon, the Royal Society of Literature was virtually founded.

The King not only became its patron, he assigned it 1,100 guineas a year as pensions for ten Royal Associates, and a prize for a dissertation. 'As the Founder and Patron of this Society,' wrote a contemporary, 'the King presents himself to his People, singly, as the Friend of Letters, as an example of Munificence, and the Promoter of what has long been wanting to the Literary credit of the Country.' The Society hoped 'to unite and extend the general interests of literature; to reward literary merit by patronage; to excite literary talent by premiums; and to promote literary education . . .'.

One might have thought that such proposals were beyond criticism; but there were still people who objected that controversial topics might be raised under cover of literary discussion, and that the Society might be made a dangerous political instrument. There were more frivolous objections. In June 1825, the Council of the Royal Society resolved unanimously to oppose 'the application of the society calling itself the Royal Society of Literature for a charter'; the designations and titles of this new body, so they said, would undoubtedly 'interfere' with their own. However, three months later, the Royal Society of Literature received its Charter of Incorporation.

It was a royal society in more senses than one—for the Dukes of York, Clarence, and Cambridge had been the first Fellows enrolled after the King. And, more significant, the Society represented a civilization in which that unhappy phrase 'the two cultures' was unknown. The first president was, of course, the Bishop of St. David's; the first vice-presidents included the Lord Chief Justice, a surgeon, and an orientalist; among the councillors was the sculptor Francis Chantrey, whose statue of George IV now stands in Trafalgar Square. John Murray— Byron's publisher—and John Nash, the King's favourite architect, were among the early members; and one of the first Royal Associates was Coleridge (who chose to forget his personal criticism of the King, and to lecture on Æschylus). In 1827, the Society awarded one of its gold medals to Sir Walter Scott. It was Scott's son-in-law, the journalist John Gibson Lockhart, who collected his medal for him. 'It is a very pretty thing,' Lockhart reported. He added—I regret to say—'such twaddle as [the Society's] proceedings . . . I really did not believe could exist in any Christian land.'

It must be said that in the relationship between Sir Walter Scott and the King, it was the King who showed to most advantage. When, in April 1820, he conferred a baronetcy on Scott, he said: 'I shall always reflect with pleasure on Sir Walter Scott's having been the first creation of my reign.' When, a year later, Scott came to Court, the King treated him with great distinction; and he commanded him to sit to Sir Thomas Lawrence for a portrait. As for Scott, he blandly informed his son: 'I hope my glimpse of Court favour may be useful to your pursuits and views. For myself it is all one.'

Sir Walter had every intention of assuring the future. In 1822, when he organized the King's state visit to Scotland, he was roundly criticized for his own ostentatious part in the proceedings. 'It is a pity', wrote a journalist, 'that the author of *Waverley* should deem it important to figure in every part of a corporation pageant. . . .' 'You are aware *strictly inter nos* that my interest lies Windsor ways,' Scott explained to Lockhart, 'but the art is to know how the lever should be applied.'

His hand was never far from the lever. He presented 'a most valuable Scottish history' to the King's friend and counsellor, Sir William Knighton. When an admirer in New South Wales sent him a couple of emus (which proved, to his horrified surprise, to be 6 feet high), he tried to transfer the birds to the Royal Menagerie (alas, His Majesty seemed to be provided). When his *Life of Napoleon* appeared, he 'caused a copy to be laid on the table of His Majesty's library'. At last he applied the lever boldly, and asked Knighton for advice on his son's career. The King recommended Charles Scott for the first available vacancy in the Foreign Office. Scott had known how to work the Windsor machine.

Scott was undoubtedly the writer on closest terms with the King; but among the authors whom the King most enjoyed was Jane Austen. One only wishes that they had met—one would like Miss Austen's comments on the King; one would also relish the King's observations on this brilliantly shrewd woman. Yet, though they did not actually meet, the Regent and Jane Austen were brought together by a curious chance, almost at the end of her short life.

In the autumn of 1815, when *Emma* was in the press, Jane Austen received the only mark of distinction that was ever bestowed upon her. She was nursing her brother Henry through a dangerous fever in London. Henry Austen was attended by one of the Regent's doctors, and the doctor learned that the patient's nurse was the author of *Pride and Prejudice*. Accordingly, one day, he told the gratified Miss Austen that the Regent greatly admired her novels, that he kept a set in each of his residences, and that he repeatedly read them. He had therefore informed the Regent that Miss Austen was in town, and the Regent had commanded his librarian to call on her.

Next day, the ubiquitous Mr. Clarke bustled round to invite Miss Austen to Carlton House. He had, he said, instructions to show her the library, and to pay her every attention. He had also been commanded to say that Miss Austen was at liberty to dedicate a novel to the Regent.

Dear Sir [Miss Austen instructed her publisher]
    As I find that *Emma* is advertised for publication, I think it best to lose no time in settling all that remains to be settled. . . .
    The Title page must be Emma, Dedicated by Permission to H. R. H. the Prince Regent—And it is my particular wish that one set should be completed and sent to H. R. H. two or three days before the Work is generally public. . . .

On 27 March 1816, from the Pavilion at Brighton, on the eve of Princess Charlotte's marriage to Prince Leopold of Coburg, Clarke returned the Regent's thanks 'for the handsome copy you sent him of your last excellent novel'. ('Whatever he may think of my share of the work,' wrote Miss Austen to her publisher, 'yours seems to have been quite right.') Clarke's letter must have delighted her as a piece of unconscious self-portraiture.

Pray, dear Madam, [he had written] soon write again and again.

Lord St. Helens and many of the nobility, who have been staying here, paid you the just tribute of their praise.

The Prince Regent has just left us for London; and having been pleased to appoint me Chaplain and Private English Secretary to the Prince of Coburg, I remain here with His Serene Highness and a select party until the marriage. Perhaps when you again appear in print you may chuse to dedicate your volumes to Prince Leopold: any historical romance, illustrative of the history of the august House of Coburg, would just now be very interesting.

Miss Austen had encountered a character worthy of one of her novels. She answered with an honesty and insight which were no doubt lost on him:

My dear Sir,

. . . I could no more write a romance than an epic poem. . . . No, I must keep to my own style and go on in my own way; and though I may never succeed again in that, I am convinced that I should totally fail in any other.

As Virginia Woolf would write, years later, in her essay on Jane Austen: 'The Prince Regent and his Librarian had run their heads against a very formidable obstacle; they were trying to tamper with an incorruptible conscience, to disturb an infallible discretion.'

Sir Astley Cooper, the surgeon, who knew the Regent in later life, recalled that he often woke early, and read from 5 or 6 in the morning till 9 or 10; 'and thus he became acquainted with all the new books, which he read of every description—novels, pamphlets, voyages, travels, plays—and he liked to talk of them'. He discussed political satire with Croker, he approved of Southey's article on the Catholics in the *Quarterly Review*, and he enjoyed Lady Morgan's substantial Irish novels: indeed, he was angry with Croker for criticizing her novel *Florence Macarthy*. ('Damn blackguard, to abuse a woman, isn't it?') He seems to have read all four volumes of *The O'Briens and the O'Flahertys*, soon after it appeared in 1827, for Lady Charleville informed the author: 'The King, I find, was very interested in the lighter parts; but some of the charges against the Irish government, he said, were too bad, while God knows they were not half bad enough to my mind.'

Few English monarchs seem to have taken such wide and constant pleasure in literature as George IV. As a boy, he had assured his tutor: 'Your good instruction will never be effaced from my heart.' As an elderly man, almost blind from cataract, he appointed an actress to read him English drama. His surgeon maintained that he could 'quote the beauties of almost all the works, in prose or verse, of English literature'. And since he is said to have spoken French and German as well as he spoke English, it was not surprising that he appreciated Mme de Staël, or promised to be a founder-subscriber if the Comédie-Française sent a permanent company to London. He wanted to have a French theatre licensed in London, but the Lord Chamberlain warned him that such an institution would cause anti-French riots.

The King's love of literature could be seen in many ways. He presented his father's library—over 65,000 volumes—to the British Museum, and the King's Library, a building 'worthy of the taste and dignity of the nation', was built to house the impressive collection. When a Latin work, under Milton's name, was discovered in the State Paper Office, it was translated and handsomely published by the King's command. When William Godwin, the author of *Political Justice*, asked Sir William Knighton to help enlist one of his brothers at the Charterhouse, he was, he said, encouraged to do so by 'your intimacy with the generous prince who now fills the throne'. The King approved this petition from the father-in-law of Shelley—the poet who had once dismissed him as 'that crowned coward and villain'. In 1826, when Scott was involved in financial disaster, the King was said to have shown real concern. '*This* I can well believe,' wrote Scott in his diary, 'for the King, educated as a prince, has nevertheless as true and kind a heart as any subject in his dominions.'

In the spring of 1830, Scott was gravely ill, and asked to resign the office of a principal Clerk of Session at Edinburgh.

Having received so many marks of distinction from his Majesty, I may [he wrote] be permitted to hope his uniform benevolence towards me will dispose him to concern himself in some degree, whether the old *littérateur* whom the King has delighted to honour shall continue to turn the wheel till he die in harness, or shall be allowed a remission from his labours. . . .

The King was certainly concerned. Scott—the admirer of the Stuarts—was asked to head a new commission to examine and edit the Stuart papers. The task could hardly have been chosen with more understanding. The offer must have touched his heart, and he accepted gladly. According to Lockhart, he was also offered the rank of Privy Councillor, but refused it on the grounds of his failing health and diminished fortune. The King's

last marks of friendship for Scott showed the warmth and
sympathy which he had shown, now, for some fifteen years;
and even the kindness of William IV, who would lend the
dying novelist a frigate in his final search for health and the sun,
'must not make me forget', so Scott would write, 'what I owe
to the memory of George IV, who permitted me to call him a
personal friend'.

The King's final gesture of friendship to Scott was made in
1830: the year of his own death. 'The whole day of pleasure
was damped by the news of the King's death', Scott noted in his
diary on 27 June; and, writing to Wordsworth a few days later,
he added:

Dearest Wordsworth,
    Here is a new reign which may bring hope to many—but to me
only the sad recollection that the late King was very civil to me.

The King's education had cultivated his taste, and given him
respect for scholarship; it had given him not only a knowledge
of languages, ancient and modern, but—far more important—
an active interest in literature. Dr. Markham, his tutor, had
perhaps inspired his lively interest in the classics, and led him
to patronize the Herculaneum Mission. Dr. Markham and
Dr. Hurd had no doubt helped to foster his enthusiasm for
French literature and modern history. But it was his own
generous character quite as much as his education which had
made George IV the benefactor of literature: which had led
him to support the Royal Literary Fund, to give his father's
library to the nation, and to found our own Society. Byron
respected his taste and knowledge; Shelley and Hazlitt, who
condemned him, knew little of his character, his thoughtful
affection for human beings, his respect for intelligence, his love
of wit and imagination, his own imaginative warmth of heart.
Some men of letters turned against him out of sheer perversity;
some dismissed him for his political principles, for his treatment
of his unbalanced wife, and even—strange though it may seem—
for his patronage of the arts, which seemed to them unnecessary
extravagance.

All the efforts which can be made, [wrote William Cobbett, the
radical journalist, in his Life of George IV] will never make English-
men painters and poets and musicians. . . . All that can be done, in
England, by squandering upon galleries and museums, is to excite
a desire in the vain and frivolous part of the nation to hanker after
such things.

George IV has always suffered from the philistines.

# COLERIDGE AND THE ROYAL
# SOCIETY OF LITERATURE

*By* GEORGE WHALLEY, M.A., PH.D., F.R.S.C., F.R.S.L.

*(Part of a lecture, entitled 'The Unseen Coleridge', read 23 May 1968)*
*Frank Kermode, M.A., F.R.S.L., in the Chair*

THE proposal for a Royal Society of Literature was made informally to King George IV by Bishop Burgess in 1821. The King approved of the idea and offered to support the Society with a substantial gift from the Privy Purse. The King's munificent offer was announced and widely applauded: 1,100 guineas a year, for annual grants to ten Royal Associates and an annual prize for an essay. The King actually intended no more than an outright gift of 1,000 guineas and an annual sum of 100 guineas. The public interest in the announcement was so widespread and the applause of the royal generosity so fervent that the King agreed not to rectify the Bishop's mistake. In May 1822 a provisional council was formed to prepare a constitution and regulations; these were submitted to the King and endorsed by him on 2 June 1823. The first meeting of the Society was called a few days later to appoint the Council of the Society, and the Council first met on 21 June 1823; the first Ordinary Meeting was held on 5 November of the same year.

The first Annual Meeting was called on 16 May 1824, the main item of business being the matter that had engaged the energies of Council for almost a year—the appointment of 'Ten Associates of the First Class on the Royal Foundation.' Three Royal Associates had been elected by the Council on 5 July 1823, and at a meeting on 12 February 1824 a short list of four Honorary Associates—one of them being S. T. Coleridge—was prepared from which a fourth Royal Associate was to be chosen. Coleridge already knew that Basil Montagu had recommended his name for consideration and that he was prosecuting his cause vigorously. But he was offended when he was advised by Montagu, as he told Joseph Henry Green immediately after the February meeting, 'to write to such and such & such' and so to carry out 'a regular Canvas'. He had '*jibbed*', he said, and told Montagu that 'what a man's friends did sub rosa, and what one friend might say to another in favor of an individual, was one thing—what a man did in his own name & person, was another —and that I would not, *could* not, *solicit* a single vote'. Green could if he liked drop a line to Chantrey, however. And there was one shaft of sunlight: 'One of the Electors' names is *Cattermole*!!! I wonder what twi-bestialism that Fellow committed in his pre-existent state to bring down such a name upon him!' There is no reason to suppose that the process of selection was any less impartial than it ever is in the conduct of human affairs: at their meeting on 11 March 1824 the Council chose Coleridge's name from the list of four, and Coleridge received the news a few days later in a letter signed by the Secretary of the Society, the Reverend Richard Cattermole. At the first Annual Meeting, on 1 May 1824, Coleridge—wearing a new suit for the occasion—was formally admitted Royal Associate with four others: T. R. Malthus, Sir William Ouseley, the Reverend H. J. Todd, and Sharon Turner. (Only six Royal Associates had so far been elected, and one was absent through illness.) Coleridge's undertaking to the Society is written out in full in his own hand and signed; and a draft of his brief statement of his area of interest to be explored for the Society also survives.

A Royal Associate was under only one obligation: to communicate to the Society at least one paper a year in a field of study of his own choice. The annual grant of 100 guineas was an important matter to Coleridge: it would bring him some relief from the financial anxiety that had dogged him for years. Yet before he was elected he had considered withdrawing his name because he had much work in hand—in the press, nearing completion, and in draft—which would have to be neglected if he were to meet his annual obligation; he even said that he would have withdrawn his name if he had not thought that this would embarrass his sponsors. Almost a year had passed since his election when in April 1825 he wrote to the Secretary to explain why he had not submitted a paper before, throwing himself 'upon the indulgence of the Society', and asking them to 'regard the Year past as a period employed in the liquidation of a debt previously incurred'. But he was now ready, he said, to meet his obligation for the current year, 1825, and enclosed his paper for the consideration of the committee. The selection committee acted promptly, and the paper was scheduled for almost immediate delivery.

Since Coleridge is sometimes said to be a man of unfulfilled obligations, it may be noted in passing that he was not the only

Royal Associate who had trouble with the annual paper. In the first year (1824–5), five others reneged; 1825–6—the year of Coleridge's paper—was a good year with seven Associates complying. But after that there was a sad falling off: in 1826–7 only five spoke, in 1827–8 four, in 1828–9 none, in 1829–30 four; and after the Royal Bounty was withdrawn in 1831 only one of the Royal Associates—James Millingen—continued to communicate year after year.

On 18 May 1825—a Wednesday—at 3 o'clock in the afternoon, Samuel Taylor Coleridge delivered at an Ordinary Meeting the one paper he was ever to read to the Society: 'On the *Prometheus* of Aeschylus: An Essay, Preparatory to a series of disquisitions respecting the Egyptian in connection with the Sacredotal Theology, and in contrast with the Mysteries of ancient Greece.' The Right Reverend the President (Thomas Burgess, Bishop of St. David's) was in the chair; the Secretary was present and—beyond whatever other members of the Society may have been there—a few loyal friends: Basil Montagu (Coleridge's original sponsor), Joseph Henry Green (physiologist, Coleridge's philosophical collaborator, and later his literary executor), and Edward Irving (the spellbinding preacher); James Gillman, Coleridge's host in Highgate since 1816, intended to be there and probably was. Coleridge's nephew, John Taylor Coleridge, was invited but did not make it, otherwise we might not have Coleridge's own account of the lecture:

I had to inflict an hour and 25 minutes' Essay, full of Greek and superannuated Metaphysics, on the ears of the Royal Society of Literature— . . . 'Deuce take me' (as Charles Lamb says in his 'Superannuated Man') if I did not feel remorseful Pity for my Audience all the time. For at the very best it was a Thing *to be* read not *to read*.

The minutes of the meeting simply record the title of the paper and the fact that Coleridge delivered it.

Coleridge did not continue with the 'series of disquisitions', though he seems to have sent a written apology and explanation most years and was friendly enough with the Secretary for Richard Cattermole to pay him at least one visit in Highgate. There is no sign that Coleridge consorted much, if at all, with the members of the Society, but the minutes of the Ordinary Meeting for 2 March 1831 show that he presented to the library a copy of the second edition of *Aids to Reflection* (1831) and a copy of *On the Constitution of Church and State* (1830). Both these, and a copy of the *Poetical Works*, 3 volumes, 1829, appear in the library list, but only the *Poetical Works* is still in the library. The fact that the *Poetical Works*, without autograph inscription or signature, is still in the library suggests that the other two books were inscribed by Coleridge and may have been expropriated for their association value.

The essay 'On the *Prometheus* of Aeschylus' was published by the Society but it was not exactly rushed into print. The first three parts of the *Transactions* were published in 1827, 1829, and 1832, but with no sign of Coleridge's essay. During the house-cleaning in preparation for the fourth part—vol. II, pt. ii— of the *Transactions*, the manuscript of the essay being (according to the Rules of the Society) in the Secretary's possession, the Secretary was directed on 18 December 1833 'to refer Mr. Coleridge's Memoir on the Prometheus of Aeschylus to the Writer, with a view of its being arranged for publication in a condensed form'. By that time, Coleridge was ill and his strength failing. A condensed report of the paper, prepared one imagines by Henry Nelson Coleridge, was sent to the Society but evidently was not publishable. (The text of this condensed report has, however, been preserved.) The editorial committee decided to print the complete manuscript in their possession, as can be seen by comparing the printed version with the manuscript draft from which Coleridge had worked in 1825. (The manuscript itself disappeared from the Society's archives many years ago, as did the correspondence between Coleridge and Cattermole.) Thomas J. Wise in three successive bibliographies described a separate issue of the essay, then in his possession, and now in the British Museum library: 'This Private Edition was printed and circulated in the customary manner, in advance of the reading of the Essay. Issued (in an Edition of Twenty-five copies only) stitched, and without wrappers.' This prenatal issue is sheer bibliographical fantasy. What Wise is describing is an offprint from the *Transactions*, vol. II, pt. ii of 1834 with the typographical modifications specified in the Rules of the Society: the author was entitled to twenty copies gratis. The publication ledgers of the Society show that copies of the *Transactions*, vol. II, pt. ii were sent to members on 4 July 1834, but that Coleridge was not sent one. His twenty offprints were certainly prepared: one copy is now in the British Museum (originally Wise's copy), another was reported by Wise (apparently in the possession of the Gillman family), and a third was bound in a composite volume in Joseph

Henry Green's library. But it is not certain that they reached Highgate in time for Coleridge to see them before he died on 25 July 1834.

King George IV died on 25 June 1830, but since payment to the Royal Associates was made 'on the day of the anniversary of the Society', it was not until Coleridge's grant failed to arrive in May 1831 that he realized that King William had declined to continue the Royal Bounty. Coleridge protested, and so did a few other Royal Associates. Friends protested too, both in high places and in the newspapers. Some of the public correspondence singled out Coleridge as a prime example of poverty-stricken genius suffering under royal injustice, and James Gillman had to intervene with a letter to *The Times* to relieve Coleridge of this embarrassing notoriety. But King William IV was not to be moved by compassionate pleading: he simply said that he did not have the money. Lord Grey, at the insistence of Lord Brougham, offered Coleridge £200 from Treasury funds to be paid in two annual instalments, but Coleridge declined this offer with dignity: he and the other nine had been appointed *Royal* Associates, as they understood *for life*, and a Treasury grant would be a different affair offered in a different spirit. In the end the Government invented a suitably delicate means of providing a grant for the surviving Royal Associates, but only two lived to receive their grants, and it was too late to benefit Coleridge. He could not pretend that the loss was not serious, and said shortly before his death: 'I have not been worth a shilling of my own in the world since King William IV took my poor gold chain of a hundred links—one hundred pounds—with those of nine other literary veterans, to emblazon d'or the black bar across the Royal arms of the Fitzclarences.' For the Royal Society of Literature and its officers, however, he cannot have felt anything but respect and gratitude.

PRINTED IN GREAT BRITAIN
AT THE UNIVERSITY PRESS, OXFORD
BY VIVIAN RIDLER
PRINTER TO THE UNIVERSITY